This military and historical sketch was developed to spread knowledge about the Russian-Ukrainian war and is dedicated to the Kyiv Defence Operation of 2022. Its purpose is to recreate the course of events that took place during the defence of the Ukrainian capital in February–April 2022 and to tell the story of the heroism displayed by our defenders in their struggle against the Russian aggressor.

The publication is intended for commanders (chiefs), specialists in psychological support structures for personnel in the Armed Forces of Ukraine, as well as anyone interested in the military history of Ukraine.

During the preparation of this essay, materials from the military history department of the military-strategic analysis department of the Main Operational Directorate of the General Staff of the Armed Forces of Ukraine were used.

CONTENTS

Preface

On 24 February 2022, the world awoke to a different reality.

Russia had launched its full-scale invasion of Ukraine. That day entered history as the beginning of one of the most tragic events of the 21st century. The war that had been smouldering since 2014 erupted with new force, bringing death, suffering, and destruction to millions. What humanity had hoped to leave forever in the past—mass bombings, forced displacement, and genocide against civilians—returned before our eyes. More than seven decades after the end of the Second World War, the world faced a tragedy that fundamentally changed its understanding of security and peace.

This is not merely a war of one state against another.

It is a challenge to all of civilized humanity—a struggle for values, for freedom, and for the basic right to exist.

From the very first days of the full-scale invasion, it was crucial for Ukraine to convey the truth—to show the world not only official reports or images from the news, but the real face of war. For people living in a digital reality, it is difficult to imagine what it means to live under bombardment or to lose loved ones.

For this reason, the idea arose to present the war to the world in the form of exhibitions of destroyed enemy equipment and missile fragments that had killed Ukrainians only days before—shown in European cities.

The most striking and symbolic of these exhibitions took place in Berlin.

Right in front of the embassy of the aggressor state, a destroyed Russian T-72 tank was displayed. This was made possible thanks to the courage and determination of Wieland Giebel and Enno Lenze of the Berlin Story Bunker museum. The tank had been destroyed by an anti-tank mine on 31 March 2022 during the Battle of Kyiv, near the village of Dmytrivka close to Bucha.

"This tank is our protest against the war unleashed by Russia and an expression of our solidarity with Ukraine," Giebel and Lenze declared. During the large-scale invasion they visited Ukraine several times, supporting the Ukrainian people's struggle against Russian aggression through both words and deeds.

This book is another shared step toward truth—a truth that cannot be silenced. It tells the story of the Battle of Kyiv, which became a symbol of resistance and marked a turning point in the war. In March 2022, the enemy expected to seize the Ukrainian capital "in three days" and bring Ukraine to its knees. Yet Kyiv stood firm. The professionalism of the Ukrainian Armed Forces, the strategic skill of the city's defense commander, General Oleksandr Syrskyi, and the courage of volunteers, helpers, and ordinary citizens of Kyiv and its surrounding region disrupted the Kremlin's plans.

This victory prevented the fall of Ukraine, inspired the population to continue resisting—and destroyed once and for all the myth of the "invincible Russian army."

The book was written by Ukrainian military scholars based on materials from the General Staff of the Armed Forces of Ukraine. This gives it particular value: it is not merely a narrative but a documented history written by those who experienced the war firsthand.

Special thanks are extended to Colonel Volodymyr Moroz, head of the Research Center for Humanitarian Issues of the Armed Forces of Ukraine, and Colonel Oleksii Nozdrachov, deputy head of the Central Scientific Research Institute of the Armed Forces of Ukraine, for their support in realizing this important project.

This book is more than a story of war. It is a testimony to the courage and sacrifice of the Ukrainian people. It reminds us all: freedom is not a permanent condition—it must be defended. As you read these pages, remember: the fight is not yet over, and the future of the world depends on our unity.

Hanna Maljar
Deputy Minister of Defense of Ukraine, 2021–2023

Introduction

On 24 February 2022, the Russian Federation launched a large-scale armed aggression against Ukraine, opening a new phase in a long-running war aimed at destroying our statehood and national identity. From the first days of the invasion, it became clear that the capture of the Ukrainian capital was the main goal of the Russian invaders.

In Ukrainian public discourse, the events connected to the defense of Kyiv in 2022 are known as the "Battle of Kyiv," while among military historians of the Russo-Ukrainian war, they are referred to as the "Kyiv Defensive Operation."

Chronologically, this operation lasted 38 days—from the beginning of the invasion until the complete expulsion of the occupiers from the Kyiv region on 2 April 2022. But for all who remained in Ukraine during that difficult time, these days will never be forgotten. Every Ukrainian, wherever they were, understood perfectly that by saving Kyiv, Ukraine was first and foremost defending its independence.

To defend the capital, the Armed Forces of Ukraine had to hold back the Russian invaders along a wide front on the borders with Belarus and Russia, in the regions of Zhytomyr, Kyiv, Chernihiv, and Sumy. On their way to Kyiv, the enemy met the resistance of hundreds of Ukrainian settlements—each becoming a symbol of resilience and an outpost of the unbreakable Ukrainian spirit. Their defenders became national legends: the cities of Bucha, Hostomel, Irpin, Okhtyrka, and Chernihiv among them.

In defending their freedom and independence, Ukrainians demonstrated extraordinary bravery, heroism, willpower, and self-sacrifice in the struggle against the Russian aggressor. By late March and early April, Ukrainian defenders forced the occupiers to flee the country in disgrace.

The Kremlin had clearly underestimated both the capabilities of the Ukrainian Armed Forces and the determination of the Ukrainian people to resist with weapons and defend the territorial integrity and independence of their state.

Ukraine achieved what few expected: in fierce battles against a vast horde of invaders, it not only held its ground but also won, driving the invaders out of Polissia, Sivershchyna, Slobozhanshchyna, and the right-bank part of the Kherson region.

The success of the Kyiv defensive operation laid the groundwork for future victories over the enemy. As General-Colonel Oleksandr Syrskyi, Commander of the Ground Forces of the Armed Forces of Ukraine and Commander of the Kyiv Defense, stated at the time:

"This operation has shown that we will resist with all our determination and skill. We know this is only a small episode in the overall struggle for Ukraine, but it is an extremely important one... Difficult and bloody months lie ahead. But every new morning brings us closer to the moment when there will be no Russian soldiers anywhere on the territory of Ukraine—at least, no living ones."

The authors wrote this military-historical essay on the eve of the third anniversary of the Battle of Kyiv. Sadly, many of those who prevented the enemy from capturing our capital have since lost their lives in subsequent battles for our freedom.

This modest work is dedicated to the memory of the soldiers who fell on the battlefields of Ukraine.

I. The Plans of the Russian Aggressor to Capture the Capital of Ukraine

Before launching its full-scale invasion, the Russian military command had massed more than 175,000 troops along Ukraine's borders with Russia and Belarus. In order to fulfil

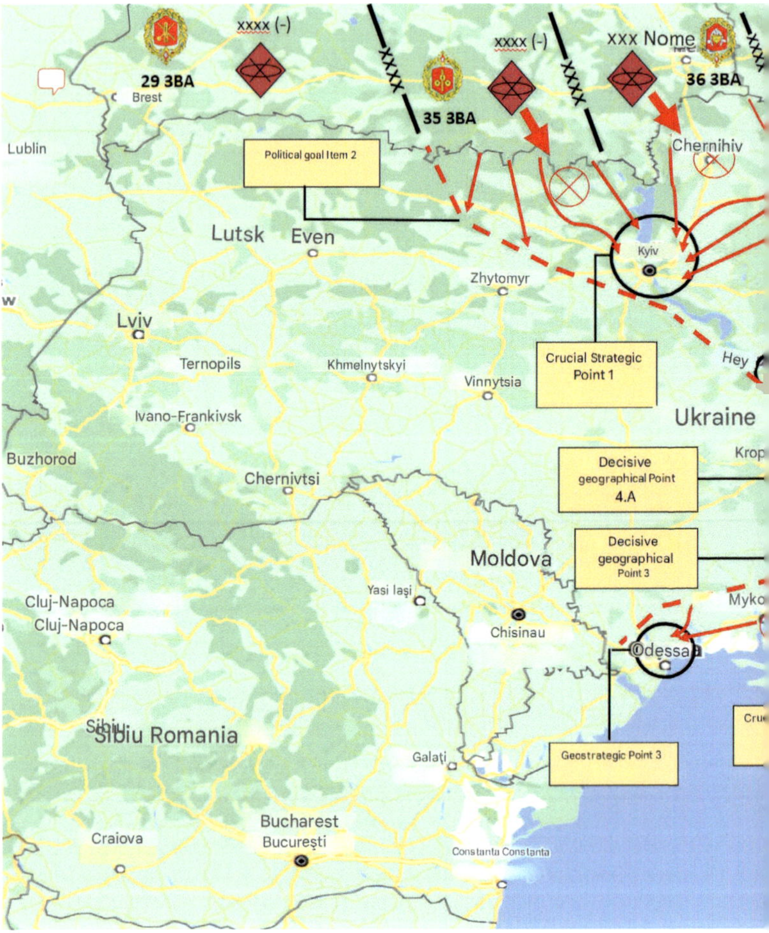

Fig. 1: Assessment of the most important strategic and operational objectives of Russian troops in Ukraine

the strategic task of capturing the Ukrainian capital, powerful Russian military groupings were established on the territories of both countries. They operated in several directions within two operational zones — Polissia and Siverskyi.

The most combat-ready and best-equipped units of Russia's Eastern Military District were concentrated in the

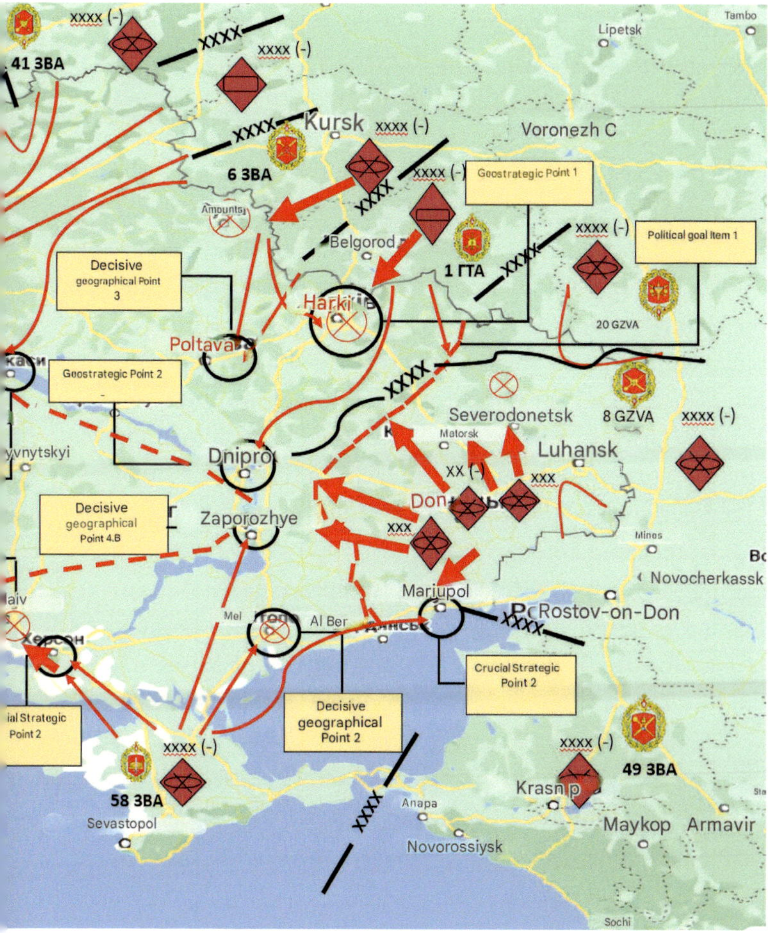

Polissia operational zone, in the Homel region of Belarus. To conduct an offensive toward Polissia, the invaders formed a group consisting of units from the 29th, 35th, and 36th Combined-Arms Armies, the Pacific Fleet, and the Airborne Forces – a total of up to fifteen tactical battalion groups.

According to the plan, these forces were to advance from Belarus toward Chernobyl – Kyiv along the right bank of the Dnipro River, seize the Chernobyl Nuclear Power Plant, gain control over the M06 Kyiv–Chop highway, and move toward the railway junction at Fastiv to enable an assault on Kyiv from the west and southwest. Forward detachments of the enemy were expected to cross that highway near Stoianka by 2 p.m. on the first day of the invasion.

Another day was allocated to encircle the capital from the south — from Makariv to Vasylkiv — and thus form an outer front around the city. Simultaneously, the Russians planned to land airborne troops at the Hostomel and Vasylkiv airfields. By doing so, they intended to block the city, its communication lines, and the command channels of Ukrainian troops; to seize weapons and ammunition depots; to spread panic among the population; and to create the conditions for special-forces units to capture television centres and government buildings — the Office of the President of Ukraine, the Verkhovna Rada, the Cabinet of Ministers, the Ministry of Defence, the General Staff, and others.

The leadership of the aggressor state assumed that the Ukrainian capital would be defended only by small, disoriented forces, confused by political chaos, and that the "Kyiv authorities" would flee. Their aim was to raise the Russian flag over all state institutions of Ukraine by the third day of the invasion. The Kremlin planned to proclaim the fall of the so-called "anti-people regime" and install a puppet "new government." Afterwards, Russian guard units were to enter the city to conduct repressive measures against the civilian population.

Particular attention was paid to the second group of Russian forces — the 36th and 41st Combined-Arms Armies, up to thirteen tactical battalion groups, which were concentrated on the opposite side of the Dnipro in Russia's Bryansk and Kursk regions (the Siverskyi operational area). This grouping was later reinforced by the 90th Tank Division of the 2nd Combined-Arms Army and was to advance simultaneously with the first (Belarusian) group toward the Brovary–Boryspil line, to blockade Kyiv from the east.

In addition, units of the 45th Special-Purpose Brigade of the Russian Airborne Forces, as well as other special-operations elements, were stationed at the Mozyr airfield in Belarus. These troops had gained experience in February 2014 during the seizure of the building of the Verkhovna Rada of the Autonomous Republic of Crimea. To conduct an airborne assault, at least 56 helicopters were deployed there. At the Russian airbases in Pskov, Ivanovo, Tver, and Ryazan, units of the 76th, 98th, and 106th Airborne Divisions were prepared for loading onto transport aircraft. Evidently, the Russians concentrated their main effort on the western strategic axis.

The enemy had also built in advance a network of informants within Ukrainian territory. At the beginning of the invasion, they positioned themselves near critical infrastructure sites and military units, took photographs, and placed "beacons" to guide air and missile strikes. Suspicious civilians were repeatedly observed along international highways, tracking the movements of Ukrainian military equipment.

It should be noted that within the first days, Ukrainian security forces neutralized twenty-three "sleeper" sabotage

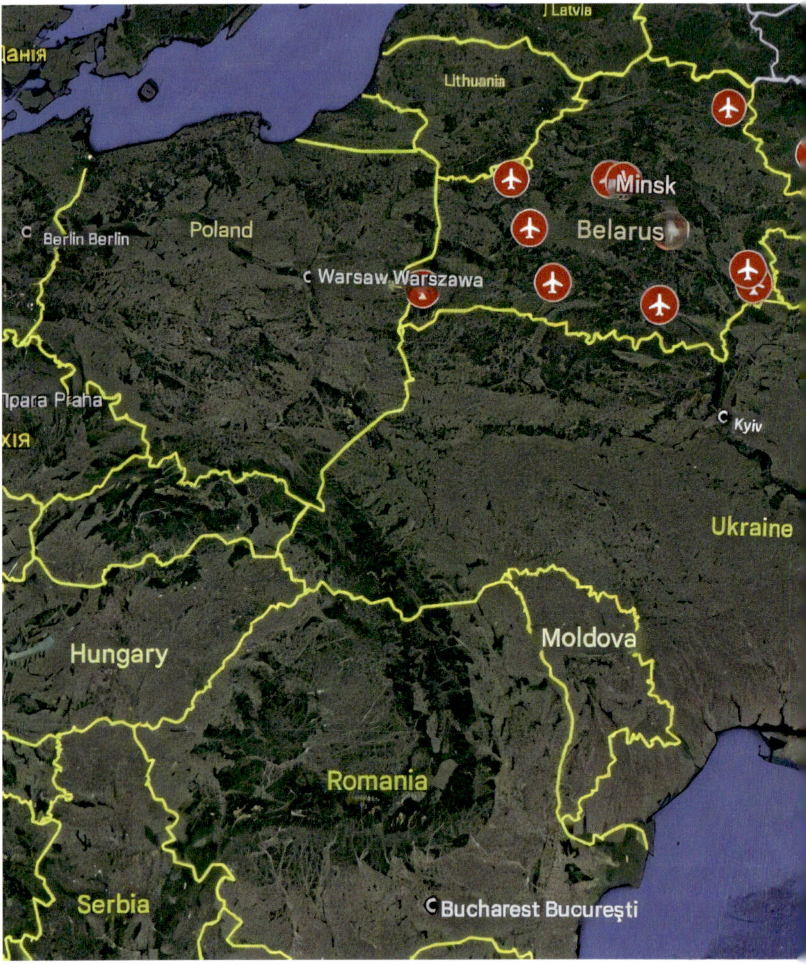

and reconnaissance groups in Kyiv. Each consisted of five to seven individuals—mostly Ukrainian citizens recruited by Russian intelligence services.

Meanwhile, the Ukrainians were preparing for defence.

Map of military airfields around Ukraine based in Belarus and Russia

II. Measures taken by Ukraine's military and political leadership to prepare Kyiv for defence

From February 10 to 20, the aggressor country conducted unscheduled military exercises in Belarus called "All-Russian Military Games 2022," during which a powerful strike force was formed.

Upon receiving intelligence about the enemy's plans, preparations for the defence of the Kyiv agglomeration began immediately. It became clear that after the exercises, the Russian contingent would remain near the Belarusian-Ukrainian border and pose a threat to our state.

Therefore, in accordance with the order of the General Staff of the Armed Forces of Ukraine, on February 12, 2022, a decision was made to establish a headquarters for the Kyiv Defence and, taking into account the real situation, a plan for the defence of the city was developed. The commander of the Land Forces of the Armed Forces of Ukraine, Colonel General O. Syrskyi, was put in charge of the defence of the capital. Since then, systematic work has begun on planning and conducting the Kyiv Defence Operation.

First, reconnaissance was carried out in the area where the enemy's invasion was expected. To defend the city, Colonel General O. Syrskyi organised two lines of defence, built taking into account natural obstacles that could hinder the enemy's advance:

Outer line – Demydiv, Huta-Mezhyhirsk, Horenka, Irpin, Bilohorodka, Bobrytsia, and Rusaniv, Hoholiv, Kalynivka, Pukhivka, and Khotianivka;

Inner line – within the administrative territory of Kyiv.

The length of the outer line was 150 km, and the inner line was 88 km. Based on the available forces and resources, the defence was organised only from the north and west.

At the same time, the inner defensive line needed to be re-equipped in an extremely short time, and air defence

Commander of the Land Forces of the Armed Forces of Ukraine – Commander of the Kyiv Defence, Colonel General Oleksandr Syrskyi

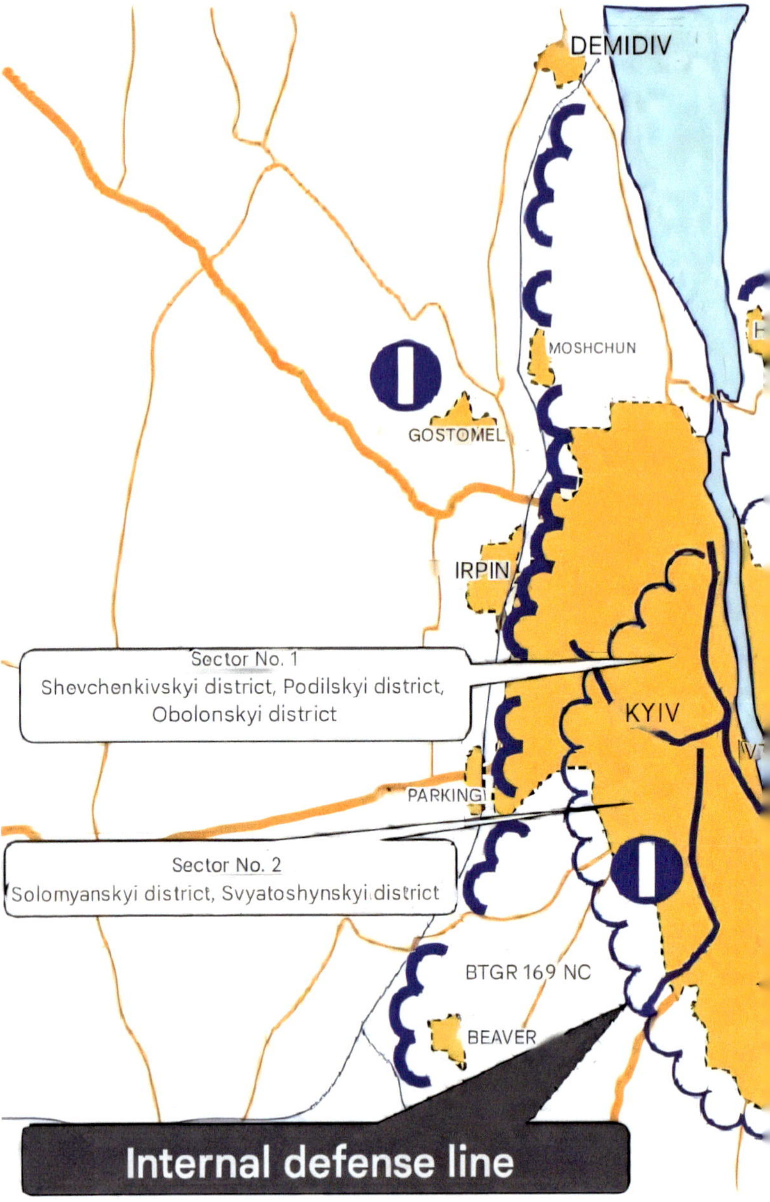

Fig. 2: Defensive lines and sectors of Kyiv

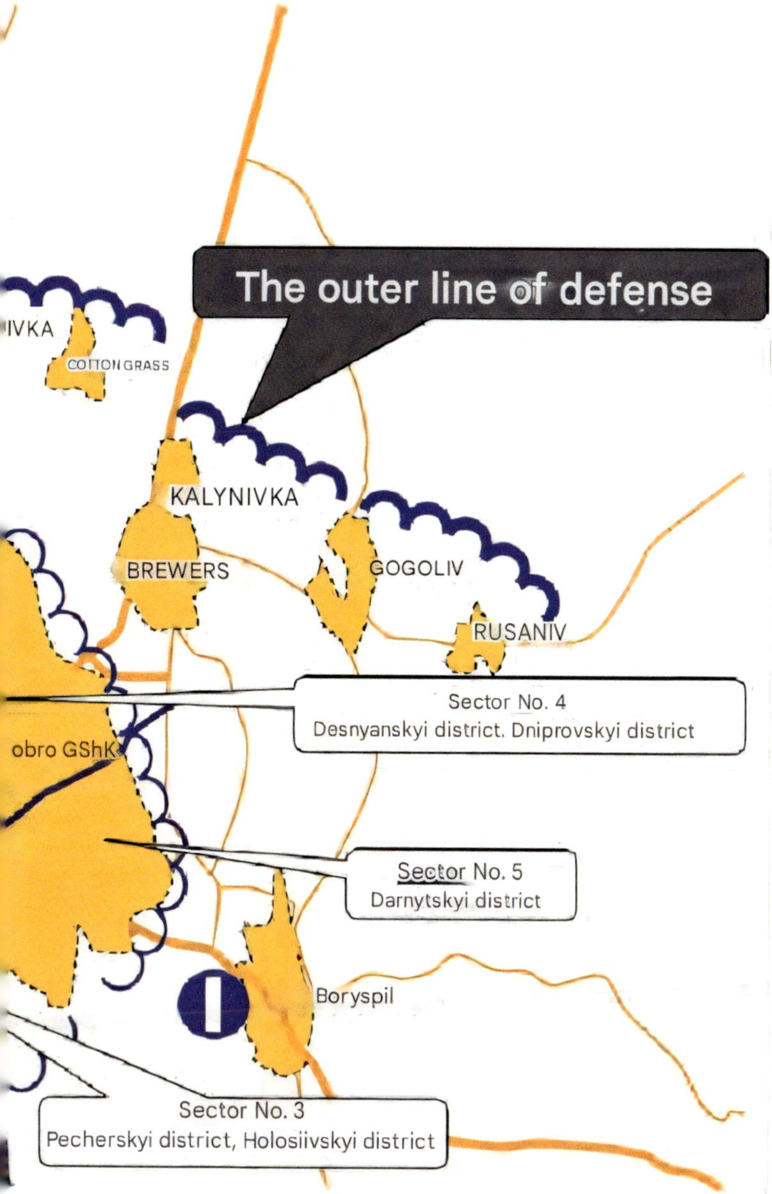
The outer line of defense
IVKA
COTTON GRASS
KALYNIVKA
BREWERS
GOGOLIV
RUSANIV
Sector No. 4
Desnyanskyi district. Dniprovskyi district
obro GShK
Sector No. 5
Darnytskyi district
Boryspil
Sector No. 3
Pecherskyi district, Holosiivskyi district

systems, aviation, helicopters, and artillery had to be protected from the first enemy strike from the air. It was planned to create an outer ring of defence as far as possible from the inner ring in order to protect the central part of the city from shelling and prevent the Russians from fighting on the approaches to Kyiv. Under these circumstances, the enemy had to be within range of our artillery. As time showed, this plan proved to be successful, and the historical experience of 1941 helped us a lot.

The city and later the region were divided into sectors.

Their number and functions were subsequently refined and changed. The sectors were tasked with preparing for the circular defence of the city by holding strongholds, checkpoints, important areas, facilities, and structures; organising fortifications for strongholds, checkpoints, command posts for the Troops of the Operational Command, district and city administrations, and volunteer formations of territorial communities; equipping checkpoints on main roads with concrete barriers, mines, and other obstacles that would prevent the passage of any enemy equipment; organising cooperation between military units (subunits) and local self-government bodies (military administrations) to ensure the high-quality and timely fulfilment of assigned tasks.

Constant communication was established between the sectors headed by the heads of structural units of the Command of the Land Forces of the Armed Forces of Ukraine. To ensure effective work, appropriate headquarters were deployed, staffed by experienced military personnel, mainly officers from the National Defence University of Ukraine and other higher military educational institutions and training (educational and training) centres (units). These military educational institutions and centres created combat units. Secondly, for the successful operation of defence forces and assets, the functions of state executive bodies in the city and region were distributed.

Thus, the Kyiv City Military Administration (headed by Major General M. Zhyrnov, appointed on March 1) and the headquarters of the Kyiv Troop Area (headed by Colonel O. Pavlii, commander of the 112th Troop Brigade) were responsible for supplying the units.

Defence on the outer borders of the city and within the region was organised by the Kyiv Regional Military Administration, which was later headed by the commander of the Joint Forces, Lieutenant General O. Pavliuk.

Colonel General O. Syrskyi exercised direct control over all allocated forces and resources. To ensure coordination between the command structures and the various security and defence forces of Ukraine, appropriate operational groups were deployed at the joint command post.

Thirdly, one day before the likely invasion of Russian troops, the commander of the Kyiv defence forces held a coordination meeting, which was attended by the heads of the defence forces of Ukraine whose forces and resources were involved in the defence of the capital, as well as representatives of the Kyiv City State Administration and the heads of district state administrations. At the meeting, the plan for the defensive operation, the order of its conduct, and the organisation of cooperation were agreed upon, and the composition of the heads of the sectors created was announced. Since then, the composition of the Kyiv Defence Council has also been determined, which subsequently included representatives of the region. These measures subsequently played a decisive role in the defence of the capital.

Fourth, during the planning of the operation, some elements of the 1941 Kyiv fortified area were used, and the trenches and dugouts of the city's defenders at that time were cleared and deepened.

During the Russian shelling in February–March, some of the fortifications from the 1940s were used by our troops and local residents as shelters.

For example, the former command post in the Bilohorodka district and the fortifications in Romanivka. They served as bomb shelters, but it was not always possible to use them for observation or firing, as the surrounding area was densely overgrown or heavily built up.

Troop units also used the remains of Wehrmacht positions from 1943, particularly on the Windy Hills near Taras Shevchenko Square in Kyiv.

Fifth, even before the enemy invasion, several land forces were created, and after the start of the Russian offensive, they were reinforced: from the north – a group of forces and means of Kyiv Defence, from the north-

Fortifications of the Kyiv fortified area during World War II

west – the Volyn operational group, and from the north-east – the Siversk group.

Taking responsibility, Colonel General O. Syrskyi moved part of the forces and means of the Kyiv Defence in advance to the very positions and directions where the enemy's attack was expected: the northeast and north-west, that is, from the areas of Chernobyl and Chernihiv.

The 72nd Mechanised Brigade formed the core of the Kyiv defence group on the outer line. On February 21, its units advanced towards Kyiv.

The main Russian attack was expected from the Chernihiv direction, so the brigade's main forces were located there. On the other flank, on the right bank of the Dnieper, there were only infantry units. At the same time, the forces and resources of this brigade were insuffi-

A column of the 72nd Motorised Rifle Brigade advancing to its positions

cient, covering only a quarter of the minimum defence requirements.

Therefore, Colonel General O. Syrskyi decided to create combined rifle battalions from the personnel of higher military educational institutions and military training units (centres). The defence of the capital was also reinforced by the 101st Brigade of the General Staff of the Armed Forces of Ukraine, the 214th OP-FOR Brigade (ODShBR – Separate Airborne Assault Brigade), and two BTGs, Battalion Tactical Groups, from the 169th National Centre. The combined units underwent combat training while performing combat tasks.

However, the defenders of the capital experienced an acute shortage of artillery, which was concentrated at that time mainly in eastern Ukraine.

The Chief of Artillery of the Land Forces of the Armed Forces of Ukraine, who was responsible for the artillery support of the Kyiv Defence, had only a combined artillery group at his disposal.

Therefore, to strengthen the Kyiv Defence, in accordance with the decision of the commander of the Kyiv defence, artillery systems that were normally used in the training process as well as nine heavy long-range 2S7 Pion artillery guns from the 43rd Airborne Artillery Brigade, which formed a combined division. The artillerymen were ordered to take up defensive positions outside the capital, to the northeast and northwest of the city, in areas where a Russian offensive was likely. On February 24, units of this brigade marched 120–140 km.

2S7 Pion heavy long-range artillery gun

All available forces were mobilised to defend the capital on the inner line, including units from the National Guard of Ukraine, the State Border Service of Ukraine, the National Police of Ukraine, as well as units that were still being formed on February 24. There were many people willing to defend the country, including many with combat experience.

First and foremost, it was necessary to accomplish the most important task—to combine units with different combat command standards, weapons, and types of training with the existing units of the Armed Forces of Ukraine for their effective use. In other words, it was necessary to find a place for each unit where it could perform its assigned tasks effectively. There was very little time to do this.

At that time, the Territorial Defence units were in the final stages of formation and lacked material and technical resources and means of communication. There was virtually no time to conduct combat coordination with them. Some of the personnel were undergoing training at training centres at that time. Some of the existing weapons and military equipment were outdated, so everything available had to be used to defend the state. The existing units were severely lacking in much-needed specialists in sabotage.

In addition, there were a large number of important facilities in the Kyiv region, so significant forces and resources had to be allocated to protect them.

Sixth, almost a week before February 24, all command posts of the Kyiv defenders were moved to likely directions of the Russian advance. Air defence of the capital was planned to be carried out within the overall air de-

Preparation of Troop units in Kyiv

fence system by a group of air forces in cooperation with the relevant units assigned to defend Kyiv.

To this end, the locations of air defence assets were changed, while aircraft were moved to reserve airfields and abroad. That is why, on the first day of the large-scale Russian invasion, enemy missiles did not find a single one of our fighter jets or military transport aircraft at their regular airfields.

The preparation of the capital for defence was carried out quite secretly. Even a high-ranking representative of the US Department of Defence noted that Washington knew more about the Russian invasion plan than about the Ukrainian defence plan.

Seventh, the Command of the Armed Forces of Ukraine planned the Kyiv Defence Operation, the main method of which was to systematically destroy enemy groups on the approaches to the city. The main efforts of the Defence Forces in this operation were focused on repelling the Russian offensive through active combat operations while conducting manoeuvre defence. At the same time, it was planned to strike the enemy with air strikes, artillery fire, and the use of general military reserves in combination with a system of engineering barriers and mobile reserves. Particular importance was attached to measures aimed at preventing the landing of air (river) assaults.

III. The beginning of the large-scale invasion of the Russian federation in the north-western operational zone

At 04:30 on February 24, the enemy launched an air offensive operation, during which it began shelling our important (critical) facilities in order to reduce the intensity of resistance and demoralise the population.

Our military and civilian airfields were hit by air, sea, and ground-based cruise missiles and the onboard weapons of enemy army aviation helicopters: Boryspil, Kramatorsk, Chuhuiv, Starokostiantyniv, Kulbakine, Lutsk, Ozerne, Ivano-Frankivsk, Brody, Mirgorod, military warehouses, command posts, air defence system facilities and radio-electronic reconnaissance facilities, etc.

In the Kyiv direction, from 04:30 to 05:00, the invaders launched missile strikes on the Boryspil airport, units of the

Advance of a Russian military convoy across the state border of Ukraine

Operational zones where the armed aggression of the Russian federation was repelled

Special Operations Forces, Air Defence Forces, Radio Technical Forces, the 39th air defence missile battery (Mezhyhiria) and the 1st Brigade of the National Guard of Ukraine (Novi Petrivtsi).

At the same time, in the Kyiv, Chernihiv, and Sumy directions, the enemy began to advance from the starting areas of battalion tactical groups.

Russian invaders crossed the state border from the Zhytomyr border guard detachment (border guard units “Ovruch,” “Vychivka,” “Mlachivka,” ‘Ivankiv’), Chernihiv border guard detachment (border guard units “Dereviny,” Semenivka, Hirske, Hremiach, Dobrianka, Dniprovske) and the Sumy border guard detachment (border guard units in Velyka Pysarivka, Yunakivka, Nova Sloboda). Our border guards were the first to engage in combat with the superior forces of the enemy.

On the first day of the large-scale invasion of Russian troops into our territory, several operational zones were formed in which the Armed Forces of Ukraine organised countermeasures against the aggressor, in particular the North-Western zone within the northern part of the Zhytomyr, Kyiv, Chernihiv, and Sumy regions.

According to the enemy's plan, its main efforts were focused on striking the Polissia Operational Area. In the Siverskyi Operational Area, Russian troops were to pin down our units to prevent their redeployment to the Polissia Operational Area, as well as block or capture large settlements and key logistics hubs. The Russian troops were to advance in marching columns at maximum speed, deploying into combat formations only in case of a threat of encountering strong resistance from the defence forces of Ukraine.

IV. Zurückdrängen der Offensive der Streitkräfte der Russischen Föderation im Operationsgebiet Polissia

The advance of Russian troops in the Polissia Operational Area began with an airborne operation. At 11:00 a.m. on February 24, 18 Mi-8 helicopters of the Russian Armed Forces appeared in the sky over Hostomel, transporting paratroopers from the 45th Special Forces Brigade. They crossed the Belarusian-Ukrainian border and approached the Antonov state-owned aircraft manufacturing plant at low altitude along the Prypiat River. Sixteen Ka-52 Alligator attack helicopters provided cover for the enemy airborne assault. Almost 300 Russian paratroopers attempted to take control of the runway and control tower to ensure the further landing of their main forces, which were to arrive on Il-76 transport aircraft. It should be noted that Ukrainian units guarding the airfield were ready to repel the enemy attack.

Aircraft parking area at Antonov State Enterprise airport, Hostomel, littered with debris from downed Russian helicopters

During the landing, enemy fire support helicopters brazenly circled 15–20 meters above the ground and carried out several raids on the positions of the fire units of the National Guard's of Ukraine company tactical group. Our defenders included two anti-aircraft gun crews stationed at the airfield and two crews with Igla man-portable air defence systems. It should be noted that the day before the invasion, the location of our air defence systems had been changed, so they remained unknown to the Russians. It was these systems that fired effectively at the enemy's aircraft. However, immediately after the MANPADS were launched, Man-Portable Air Defence System, their positions came under machine gun fire from an enemy sabotage and reconnaissance group.

During the attack on the airfield, its defenders included: units of the 4th Brigade of the National Guard of Ukraine (mainly brigade command officers and conscripts), as well as border guards and firefighters who worked there. The main forces and military equipment of the brigade were moved to the Luhansk region, to the area of the Joint Forces Operation, for rotation of units prior to the large-scale invasion. At the same time, a unit of special forces of the Main Intelligence Directorate of the Ministry of Defence of Ukraine was attached to the forces defending the airfield.

Throughout the day, intense fighting continued between the units guarding the airfield and enemy paratroopers, with the use of aviation and artillery. Through the joint efforts of our defenders, six enemy helicopters were destroyed (three Ka-52s and three Mi-8s). Only when the defenders of the airfield ran out of ammunition did they retreat.

Subsequently, our artillery and aviation struck the airfield runway, rendering it unusable for 18 Russian military transport aircraft Il-76 with troops, which were already in the air over Belarusian territory. Russian paratroopers were forced to march to Hostomel on armoured vehicles through the Chernobyl exclusion zone.

Realising the critical importance of preventing the enemy from capturing the Hostomel airfield, our military leadership decided to regain control of it by landing a tactical airborne assault and using anti-airborne reserves.

Three Mi-8 helicopters, which took off from Zhytomyr-Smokivka airport, landed paratroopers who engaged in a counterattack against the enemy.

As a result of fierce fighting, as of 21:00, our forces regained control of the airport, pushed the enemy out of its boundaries, and continued combat operations in the forests.

Wreckage of a destroyed Russian helicopter at the Hostomel Antonov State Enterprise airfield

The Russian command did not abandon its intention to seize the airport. This task was to be carried out by land forces – units of the 76th Airborne Brigade, which were marching to Hostomel through the Chernobyl exclusion zone in armoured vehicles. At around 3 a.m. on February 25, explosions were heard again near Hostomel.

Columns of invaders consisting of several enemy BTGs, Battalion Tactical Groups, were approaching to storm the airfield, and Ukrainian aviation delivered precise strikes against them. To block the Russians' advance south of the airfield, our forces effectively used Bayraktar UAVs, Unmanned Aerial Vehicles.

On the morning of February 25, the Russians made a new attempt to land troops at the airfield. One Russian Mi-8 transport helicopter managed to land at the airfield, but it was destroyed by our artillery. The enemy did not make any further attempts. At around 2 p.m. on the same day, under pressure from superior enemy forces, Ukrainian paratroopers and National Guard troops received orders to retreat, but were tasked with blocking the airfield and coordinating artillery fire on the Russians with the forces and resources at their disposal. In fact, control of the airfield remained with the enemy, but all its attempts to carry out a mass landing and establish an "air bridge" failed. The Russians had to land their planes with their troops in Belarus and advance towards Kyiv by land.

Our artillery systematically delivered powerful strikes on the positions of the occupiers. On February 27, the Armed Forces of Ukraine delivered another strike on the airfield. As a result, the runway was put out of action, making it impossible for enemy aircraft to land.

In addition, a significant number of the aggressor's personnel and military equipment were destroyed.

Thus, the resilience of the defenders of the Hostomel airfield, the successful coordination of the actions of the available units of the National Guard of Ukraine, the Special Operations Forces, the Airborne Forces, artillery, and aviation made it possible to thwart Russian plans for its quick capture and use. During the defence of the airfield, about 70 special forces and paratroopers of the so-called "elite" Russian units were destroyed.

The enemy continued its attempts to seize important objects of our state, using paratroopers and SRG, Sabotage and Reconnaissance Groups. At the same time, the occupiers intended to capture the military airfield in Vasylkiv. On February 24, they carried out massive air and missile strikes on it through-

Destroyed Russian military equipment at the Hostomel airfield

out the day. There were no aircraft on the runway at that time, so only the airfield infrastructure suffered partial damage.

Thus, the resilience of the defenders of the Hostomel airfield, the successful coordination of the actions of the available units of the National Guard of Ukraine, the Special Operations Forces, the Airborne Forces, artillery, and aviation made it possible to thwart Russian plans for its quick capture and use. During the defence of the airfield, about 70 special forces and paratroopers of the so-called "elite" Russian units were destroyed.

The enemy continued its attempts to seize important objects of our state, using paratroopers and DRG. At the same time, the occupiers intended to capture the military airfield in Vasylkiv. On February 24, they carried out massive air and missile strikes on it throughout the day. There were no aircraft

Ukrainian defender shows the beret of a killed Russian paratrooper

A building in Vasylkiv after enemy rocket and artillery strikes

on the runway at that time, so only the airfield infrastructure suffered partial damage.

On the night of February 26, Russian paratroopers attempted to capture the Vasylkiv airfield. They began storming one of the military units and important objects in the city. The occupiers tried to land troops at the airfield. In response, a Ukrainian Su-27 fighter jet destroyed a Russian Il-76 MD military transport aircraft along with the troops. Two Russian helicopters were shot down by the air defence forces. Servicemen of the 40th TA Brigade, Tactical Air Brigade, based in Vasylkiv, together with other units of the Armed Forces of Ukraine and the National Guard of Ukraine, repelled the enemy attack. Fierce fighting continued until the morning of February 27 and ended with the destruction of the Russian landing force and the liberation of the airfield.

On the same day, enemy troops were destroyed near the villages of Plesetske and Krushinka, north of Vasylkiv, as well as near the village of Tomylivka in the Bilotserkivskyi district. It is clear that the Russian command considered using the military airfield in Vasylkiv as a backup option for landing its troops in order to create a springboard for encircling Kyiv from the south-west. However, after repeated failed attempts, the enemy abandoned these plans.

All attempts by the occupiers to use their troops to capture other critical infrastructure facilities in Ukraine also proved futile. For example, on February 24, a group of Russian helicopters (up to 30 units) flew along the Kyiv Reservoir in the direction of the village of Khotianivka in the Vyshhorod district.

Their goal was to land troops to capture the dam of the Kyiv Hydroelectric Power Plant. Servicemen of the Air Defence Forces of the Armed Forces of Ukraine opened fire on them, forcing the enemy helicopters to return in the direction of Chernobyl.

The remains of a Russian helicopter that was shot down at the beginning of the large-scale invasion

The enemy repeatedly tried unsuccessfully to land river troops, particularly in the area of the dam near the village of Kozarovychi in the Vyshhorod district, in order to take control of the crossing over the Irpin River and create a bridgehead for an advance on Kyiv. Attempts by the occupiers to land troops to capture the Kyiv Hydroelectric Power Plant in Vyshhorod, in the Liutizh area, force the Dnipro River, and secure a foothold on its left bank near the village of Rovzhi. During one such attempt to land DRG on the Kyiv Hydroelectric Power Plant, our defenders destroyed three speedboats moving through the Kyiv Reservoir from the direction of Belarus. To counter the river landings, a boat detachment was formed from the National Police of Ukraine, the State Border Guard Service of Ukraine, and private boat owners as part of the capital's defence forces.

The capital's defenders prevented the enemy from capturing the Kyiv Hydroelectric Power Plant, which undoubtedly contributed to the success of the defensive operation.

Overall, the organisation of anti-landing defences during the Kyiv Defence proved to be effective. The anti-airborne reserves of the Defence Forces proved their ability to successfully resist elite units of the Russian Airborne Forces. It should also be noted that the Russians' use of tactical airborne troops without achieving air superiority proved fatal for them.

The invaders' airborne troops proved incapable of fulfilling their main task—the rapid capture and holding of important targets in the enemy's rear until the main forces arrived. Subsequently, they were used as light mechanised units on Ukrainian territory.

In the Polissia Operational Region, the enemy advanced with land forces simultaneously with the use of airborne troops. In the direction of Mozyr-Kyiv, the invaders' motorised rifle and airborne units, with forces of up to three BTGs, Battalion Tactical Groups, used a route from Belarus that was unexpected for the Armed Forces of Ukraine command—the Chernobyl exclusion zone.

They carried out a flanking maneuver through the 30-kilometer exclusion zone (through Prypiat) and advanced in the direction of Prypiat-Ivanivka-Dymer with the aim of blocking Kyiv from the north. Part of the Russian forces and equipment was used to capture and hold the Chernobyl Nuclear Power Plant. The National Guard troops guarding this dangerous facility did not engage in combat with the enemy in order "not to create a threat and not to violate the IAEA conventions, International Atomic Energy Agency, according

Kyiv Hydroelectric Power Plant

A Russian Ka-52 Alligator helicopter was shot down while covering the landing of troops in the Hostomel area

to which nuclear power plants are not objects of military aggression."

The enemy subsequently used the territory of the Chernobyl Nuclear Power Plant to set up their warehouses for material and technical resources.

To create the image of "good occupiers," Russian servicemen offered Chernobyl Nuclear Power Plant employees food as humanitarian aid, filming it on video. However, the employees refused the "help." The occupiers then dressed up in the uniforms of station employees and filmed a staged video. They continued to use the captured equipment of the NGU, the Chernobyl Nuclear Power Plant unit, to carry out sabotage activities.

The Russian military command did not care about the lives of its personnel. This is evidenced by the fact that the occu-

A military convoy of Russian troops heading for Kyiv from the Chernobyl direction

piers entered the radiation-contaminated area without personal protective equipment. Enemy equipment drove through the exclusion zone, raising radioactive dust, which was then breathed in by Russian soldiers. In addition, the occupiers began to build trenches in the most radiation-contaminated place – the Red Forest.

It is not surprising that the first death of a Russian soldier from radiation sickness was recorded on April 1, 2022.

However, the main forces of the Russian troops that entered from the Chernobyl direction, in the second half of the day on February 24, approached the village of Oran in the Vyshhorod district, where they split up.

One part of the invaders, heading through Sukholuchchia and along the Dnipro River, crossed the Teteriv River near

Oran and, with the aim of entering Kyiv, reached the line of Ivankiv-Katiuzhanka-Dymer.

After an unsuccessful attempt to cross the Irpin River near Demydiv, the enemy changed direction and began advancing towards Hostomel, trying to break through to the airfield to help their surrounded troops. Another part moved towards Ivankiv, where the main northern roads connecting the capital are located.

Another enemy column advanced towards this strategically important settlement, crossing the Ukrainian border at the Vilcha checkpoint in the morning. Our border guards engaged the enemy but were unable to prevent its further advance.

The trenches dug by the occupiers in the Red Forest of Chernobyl, the most radioactively contaminated place in the world

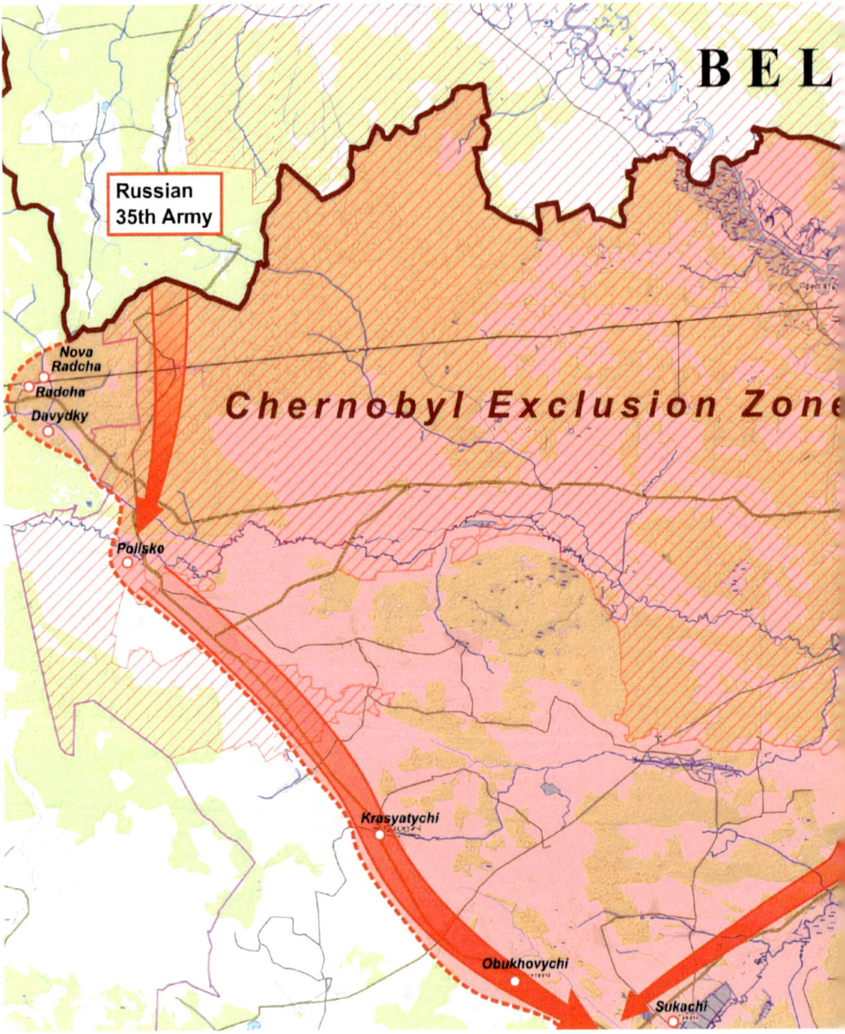

Map of the advance of Russian columns in the Kyiv direction

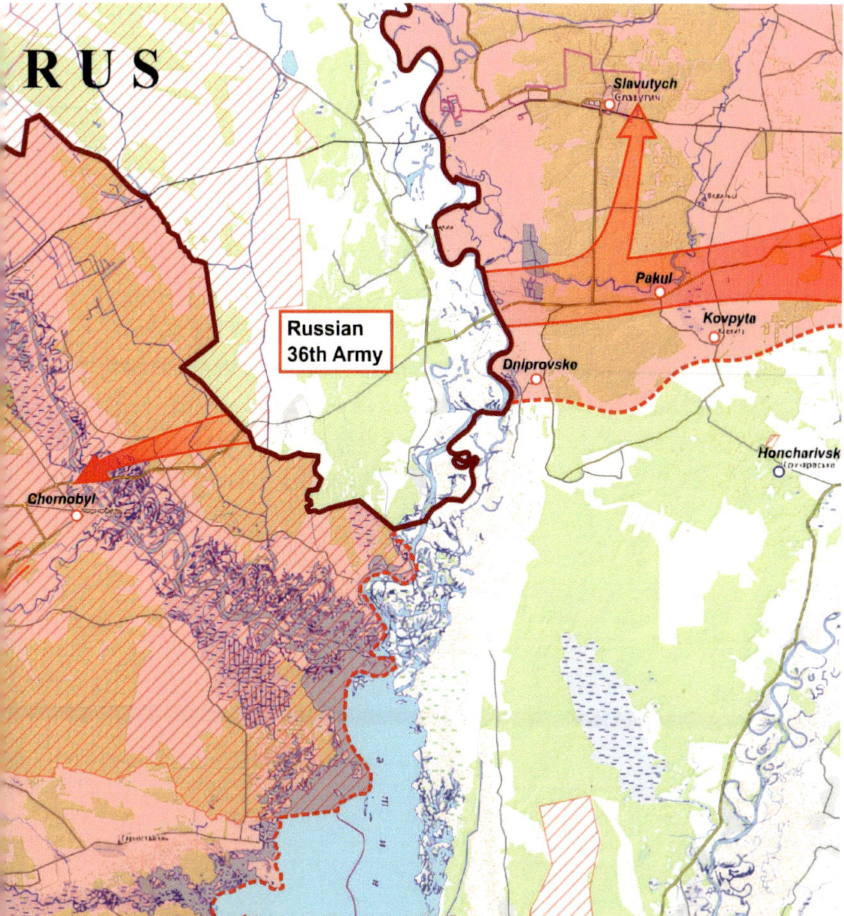
RUS
Slavutych
Pakul
Kovpyta
Russian
36th Army
Dniprovske
Honcharivsk
Chornobyl

The Kyiv Defence Operation Command decided to destroy the bridges across the Irpin and Teteriv rivers. On the night of February 25, two main bridges across the Teteriv River were destroyed near Ivankiv and near Kukhariv.

The hottest spot of the battle was the ring road near Ivankiv. Ukrainian units from the 95th Airborne Brigade and the 14th Mechanised Brigade held their defences near the towns of Dymer and Ivankiv. They managed to stop the superior enemy forces on the Teteriv River line. However, with a significant advantage in personnel and equipment, the enemy broke through our defences and continued its offensive.

Meanwhile, the enemy was building up its forces in the Polissia operational region. On the night of February 25, an-

The blown-up bridge across the Teteriv River

other enemy mechanised column of about 300 vehicles moved out of the area of concentration in the Chernobyl nuclear power plant toward the settlements of Fenevychi, Katiuzhanka, and Dymer. The enemy's equipment had no identification marks, and the columns included vehicles disguised as OSCE equipment, Organization for Security and Co-operation in Europe, presumably for the movement of DRG, Sabotage and Reconnaissance Group SRG, as well as equipment for setting up pontoon bridges.

In the Fenevychi area, this column split into three tactical groups. The first advanced in the direction of Borodianka-Makariv. Part of this group continued on to the Zhytomyr highway to encircle Kyiv from the west, while the rest continued from Borodianka along the Warsaw highway to attack Bucha and Irpin. The occupiers captured Vorzel along their route. The second group moved in the direction of Zdzhivivka – Blystavets – Antonov Airport, and the third group moved in the direction of Dymer – Demydiv – Hostomel. The last group intended to break through to Horenka, and from there, through Pushcha-Vodytsia, to Shevchenko Square in Obolon. This was the area of responsibility of Sector No. 1 of the Ukrainian forces. Thus, the Russian command tried to make maximum use of all possible logistical routes leading to Kyiv in order to transfer as many of its troops as possible to our capital.

The deputy commander of the Armed Forces of Territorial Defence Forces of Ukraine, Major General A. Barhilevich, was appointed head of the sector in this critical area. On February 24, he arrived in the village of Horenka to organise defensive lines.

Movement of Russian military columns from the Chernobyl direction towards Kyiv

Prokhoriv
Mizhrichinsky,
regional
landscape park
Progress
got scared
Dnipro river
Ostor
Gum
Tolokun
Zaliszy National
Nature Park
Yaroslavk
Vyshhorod

This area was of strategic importance due to the location of an important transport hub near the Hostomel Bridge, where three roads converge – from Hostomel, Bucha, and Irpin. The defence here was held by units of the 72nd Mechanised Brigade, the Territorial Defence Forces, the National Guard of Ukraine, and a rifle battalion of the Zhytomyr Military Institute. Due to the fact that the defenders' forces were insufficient for long-term defence and to stop the enemy's advance, a decision was made in the evening of the same day to blow up the bridge over the Irpin River near Hostomel.

At 4:00 a.m. on February 25, Major General A. Barhilevich left to conduct reconnaissance in the areas of Bucha and Hostomel. It soon became clear that Russian troops would advance towards Kyiv via the Hostomel bridge. At 08:35, a column of about 200 Russian military vehicles approached the

Destruction of a Russian military convoy on the Hostomel Bridge

Documents of a killed Russian Guard soldier

bridge. The first three white Jeeps, which were disguised as OSCE vehicles, Organization for Security and Co-operation in Europe, were deliberately allowed to pass by Ukrainian defenders.

When the main enemy vehicles entered the 138-meter bridge, they were attacked. As a result, the Russian armoured vehicles stopped and became targets for our defenders.

It was a column of Russian National Guard troops, including a combined detachment of rapid response and special forces units, which had advanced from Belarus and was moving towards Kyiv.

Topographical maps and plans of the Russian invaders, which were captured later, indicated that the occupiers did not expect intense armed resistance from the Ukrainians. In the destroyed enemy armoured personnel carriers, our defenders found ceremonial uniforms, traumatic ammunition, and rubber batons for performing police functions in the future occupied territories of Ukraine. The next day, in Hostomel, units of the National Guard of Ukraine and the Alpha special forces of the Security Service of Ukraine destroyed a column of the 141st motorised regiment of the Kadyrov Guard.

After the first battle, Ukrainian defenders blew up the Hostomel bridge and took up defensive positions from the Warsaw highway to the outskirts of Horenka in the direction of Moshchun. At the same time, in order to prevent a possible breakthrough of enemy forces to Kyiv via Pushcha-Vodytsia or the Warsaw highway, the 131st Troop began preparing a second line of defence around the intersection of roads leading to the Sviatoshyn and Obolon districts of the capital. Soon, Major General A. Barhilevich was tasked with organising the defence (almost 62 km) of the northern direction of Kyiv – from Vyshhorod to Lebedivka, Rovzh, and the Lavina shopping center.

Ukrainian defenders continued to skilfully use natural obstacles. On February 25 and 26, bridges across the Irpin River were blown up on the Zhytomyr (near the village of Stoianka) and Irpin highways, as well as in Romanivka and Demydiv. These actions allowed to gain time and bring the main forces of Ukrainian defenders to the hot spots. To block the movement of enemy forces in the direction of Demydiv – Vyshhorod – Kyiv, the capital's defence headquarters decided to blow up the dam at the entrance to the village of Demydiv in the village of Kozarovychi, which was carried out on February 25. Under these conditions, unable to move equipment across the Irpin River, the enemy attempted to advance on the positions of the 72nd Mechanised Brigade on foot and was destroyed by Ukrainian defenders.

On the roads to the capital, enemy convoys were everywhere ambushed by the Defence Forces of Ukraine. The in-

Defensive positions of the 131st Troop on the Kyiv direction

vaders approached Makarov, Hostomel, Bucha, and Irpin with significant losses in manpower and equipment.

Meanwhile, the Kyiv Defence Headquarters continuously directed the defence of the capital. Many urgent issues were resolved here, ranging from logistical support for the defence to the functioning of the capital: curfew, air raid alerts, standardisation of passes, rules for movement around the city, especially across bridges, evacuation of the population, and many other unprecedented challenges. Volunteer O. Dmitriev, with the call sign "Tikhohod," one of those who worked at the Kyiv Defence Headquarters for a month, recalled: "There was a fighting spirit at the headquarters — we will stand our ground, we must win.

This united everyone and provided great moral support. Syrskyi, who calmly and dispassionately set tasks and communicated with different people, created this atmosphere. And everything worked like clockwork. There was both iron discipline and team spirit. There was mutual respect. And everyone had enormous respect for Syrskyi."

Work was also in full swing in the five defence sectors that had been created. "We drove through all the streets and squares and, based on our knowledge of Russian military equipment, modeled where they might pass and where we needed to build defences," says Colonel Andrii Martynov, who served as chief of staff and deputy head of Sector No. 3 (Pechersk and Holosiivskyi districts) from February to April 2022. No. 3 (Pechersk and Holosiivskyi districts). "We prepared places for

The blown-up bridge across the Irpin River on the Zhytomyr highway near the village of Stoianka

Colonel General Oleksandr Syrskyi at the Kyiv Defence Headquarters, February 26, 2022

roadblocks, i.e., dump trucks loaded with sand were to go there on signal; if necessary, their wheels would be shot out so that they could not be moved by tanks or armoured personnel carriers. This was done on the main roads leading to Kyiv and in Pechersk." In addition, there were many issues to be resolved in the sectors, such as organising food supplies, establishing sanitary and hygienic conditions; deploying Troops and conducting basic training in the use of weapons, as many volunteers had never touched a weapon in their lives.

There was also a need to set up temporary storage facilities for ammunition, which had to be dispersed. As A. Martynov recalls: "All these tasks had to be performed simultaneously and immediately. And everything worked out because there was an extraordinary spirit – everyone wanted to do as much as possible, even things that were beyond their responsibility. If you saw that something needed to be done, you didn't ask for instructions from the command, you just got on with it."

In the first days of the invasion, the ranks of Kyiv's defenders were reinforced by the newly formed 112th Troop Brigade and units of the National Guard of Ukraine. In addition, units of the National Police of Ukraine, the State Emergency Service of Ukraine, and the Security Service of Ukraine, stationed in Kyiv and the region, were placed under operational control. The city was defended by lines of defence: districts, positions, checkpoints, etc.

Thus, the 72nd Mechanised Brigade, together with combined units of the 190th National Centre and the ZhVI, Zhytomyr Military Institute (S.P. Koroliov), occupied a wide strip of defence along the line: Rusaniv – Khotianivka – Demydiv – Romanivka.

Tank barriers on Independence Square in Kyiv

Training of TrO servicemen in Kyiv

The 169th NC BTG, Battalion Tactical Group, was tasked with preparing the defence area on the line Romanivka – Bilohorodka – Bobrytsia, while the 101st GSH, units of the National Guard, and the police took under their protection important military facilities, the Chaika, Sviatoshyn, and Boryspil airports, and the Kyiv Hydroelectric Power Plant. Units of the National Guard of Ukraine also set up and equipped three checkpoints in the directions of Bila Tserkva–Kyiv, Kaharlyk–Kyiv, and Berezan–Kyiv. At the same time, a combined detachment of paratroopers from the 95th Airborne Brigade took up defensive positions south of Boryspil, on the line between the villages of Revne, Hlybok, and Horodyshche. Separate battalions of the 114th Troop Transport Brigade took up positions on both banks of the Dnipro River to defend the south of the capital. The defence of the capital in this direction was also reinforced by a unit of mountain assault troops to de-

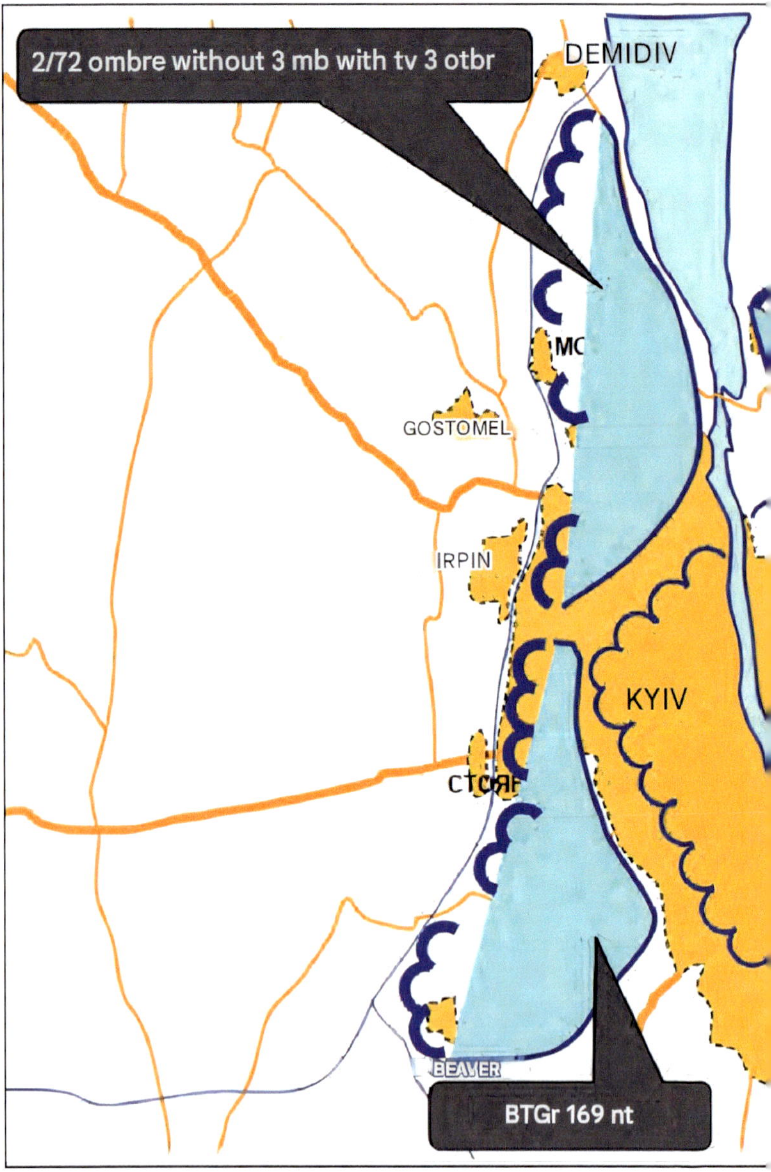

Fig. 3. Operational defence structure of Kyiv as of February 25, 2022

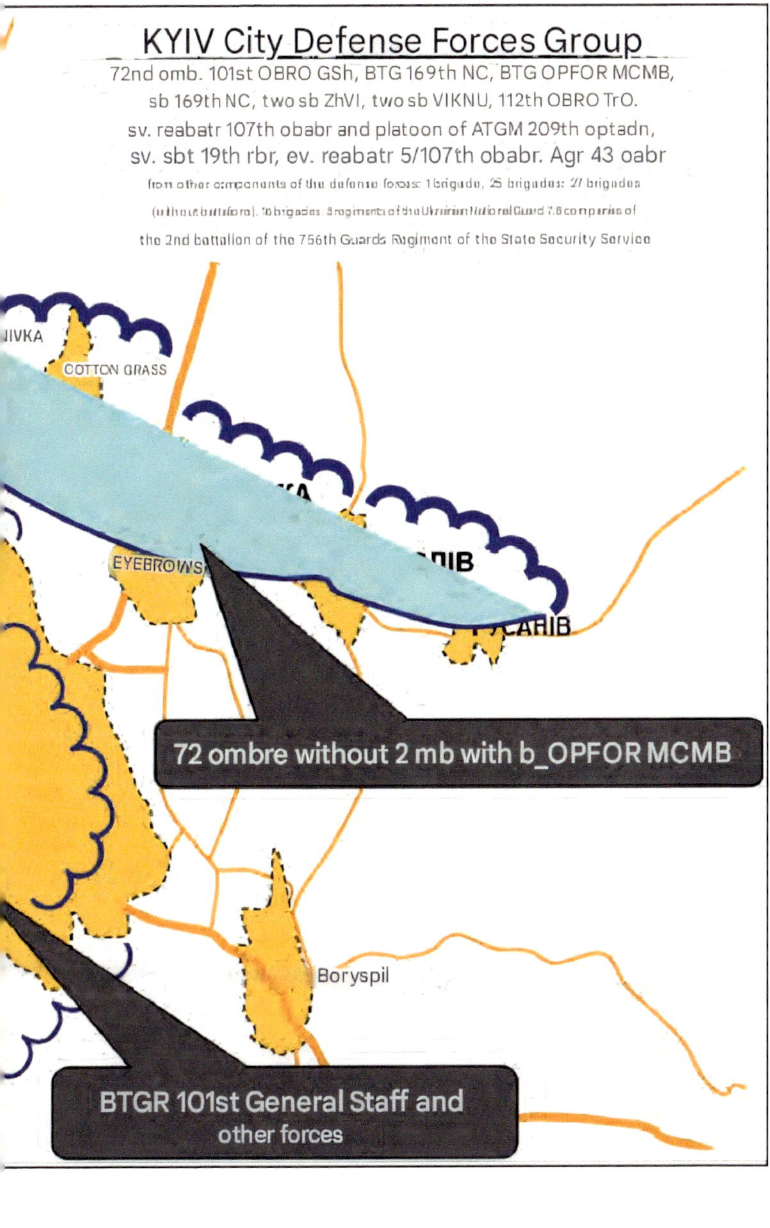
KYIV City Defense Forces Group
72nd omb. 101st OBRO GSh, BTG 169th NC, BTG OPFOR MCMB,
sb 169th NC, two sb ZhVI, two sb VIKNU, 112th OBRO TrO.
sv. reabatr 107th obabr and platoon of ATGM 209th optadn,
sv. sbt 19th rbr, ev. reabatr 5/107th obabr. Agr 43 oabr
from other components of the defense forces: 1 brigade, 25 brigades: 27 brigades
(without battalions), 10 brigades, 3 regiments of the Ukrainian National Guard 7.8 companies of
the 2nd battalion of the 756th Guards Regiment of the State Security Service
IIVKA
COTTON GRASS
EYEBROWS
CARIB
72 ombre without 2 mb with b_OPFOR MCMB
Boryspil
BTGR 101st General Staff and
other forces

Units of the National Guard of Ukraine guarded the Kyiv Hydroelectric Power Plant, airports, bridges, central heating networks, and other critical infrastructure facilities.

fend the Vasylkiv and Boryspil airports. Rifle battalions of the combined VIKNU, Taras Shevchenko Military Inst. (Kyiv), detachment took control of the Kyiv-Zhuliany International Airport and took up positions in Bortnychi. Another combined detachment from VITI reinforced the 72nd Mechanised Brigade, which was defending the capital from the northwest. VITI is the Military Institute of Telecommunications and Information Technologies in Kyiv.

The capital actively entered the defence phase. Work was carried out to block side roads from the main roads to prevent the enemy from entering the city unhindered.

Anti-tank defence nodes were set up at the entrances to the city using existing anti-tank artillery, and platoon strongholds armed with NLAW (Next Generation Light Anti-Tank Weapon, NLAW, is an anti-tank guided missile developed in

Sweden) and Javelin anti-tank missile systems (Javelin Medium Anti-Armor Weapon System is the first portable fire-and-forget anti-tank guided missile developed in the United States), Russian SPG-9 "Spear" mounted grenade launchers, and other anti-tank weapons were set up on secondary roads. Checkpoints and firing positions were set up along major roads and intersections. Mobile fire groups were created in the city's defence sectors, consisting of 5-6 servicemen and usually moving in off-road vehicles armed with machine guns and anti-tank rocket launchers. This organisation of the city's defence made it possible to quite successfully counter the actions of SRG, Sabotage and Reconnaissance Groups, and enemy tactical airborne units.

Commander of the Kyiv Defence, Colonel General O. Syrskyi, during an inspection of the organisation of checkpoints around the capital

As a result, a dense and multi-level city defence system was deployed. The structure of its management bodies was gradually improved, as well as the interaction between troops (forces) and resources and the comprehensive support system. This made it possible to quickly and effectively resolve issues related to combat, material and technical, and personnel support.

The defenders of Kyiv were in urgently need of artillery. By decision of O. Syrskyi, three BM-21 Grad multiple rocket launchers (122 mm multiple rocket launcher system, developed in the Soviet Union) from the 128th Mechanised Brigade were deployed in Novi Petrivtsi. Under constant artillery fire and rocket attacks from the occupiers in Belarus, our artillerymen fought for over a month against the forces that the enemy was pulling up to Kyiv. They literally dug into the frozen Liutizh bridgehead, where they successfully held back the Russian advance in the Vyshhorod and Irpin directions.

The average daily advance of enemy troops was up to 40 km, which allowed them to penetrate 100–120 km from the state border of Ukraine. However, seven enemy BTGs, Battalion Tactical Groups, were stopped on the approaches to the capital, on the Borodianka-Bucha-Vyshhorod line. The enemy units partially lost their combat capability and attempted to regroup. Lacking sufficient forces, the enemy was forced to bring additional units and reserves into battle prematurely.

At this line, one of its columns (over 100 armoured vehicles) from Bucha advanced to Irpin, where a unit of the 80th Airborne Brigade and local volunteers set up an ambush near the Giraffe shopping centre, destroyed 11 Russian BMD-2s, and forced the enemy to retreat. BMD-2 is a Soviet airborne infantry fighting vehicle, introduced in 1985.

A BM-21 Grad multiple rocket launcher of the 128th Mechanised Brigade strikes enemy positions

Subsequently, as a result of an artillery strike on the remnants of this enemy column, 29 North-Western ed combat vehicles and a fuel tanker were destroyed. Footage of burned enemy armoured vehicles North-Western in Bucha on Vokzalna Street Vokzalna Street went viral around the world. Ukrainian defenders continued to finish off the enemy in the city and replenished their forces with captured equipment.

On March 3, the 214th Defence Forces, together with local volunteers, took control of Bucha. The blue and yellow flag flew over the city again. But the next day, the enemy carried out a massive artillery attack and, with superior forces, pushed our forces to the eastern outskirts of Bucha. On March 5, they were forced to retreat after heavy fighting.

Subsequently, as a result of an artillery strike on the remnants of this enemy column, 29 North-Western ed combat vehicles and a fuel tanker were destroyed. Footage of burned enemy armoured vehicles North-Western in Bucha on Vokzalna Street Vokzalna Street went viral around the world. Ukrainian defenders continued to finish off the enemy in the city and replenished their forces with captured equipment.

On March 3, the 214th Defence Forces, together with local volunteers, took control of Bucha. The blue and yellow flag flew over the city again. But the next day, the enemy carried out a massive artillery attack and, with superior forces, pushed our forces to the eastern outskirts of Bucha. On March 5, they were forced to retreat after heavy fighting.

Position of Ukrainian defenders near the Giraffe shopping centre in Irpin

Destroyed column of Russian equipment in Bucha, February 27, 2022

At the same time, our units bravely defended Hostomel. For example, in the area of the Antonov airport, a group of special forces, together with local resistance groups, destroyed 20 Russian combat vehicles.

Later, on March 3, reconnaissance soldiers captured four more key intersections in Hostomel and Bucha. In total, during the battles for Hostomel on March 3–4, at least 50 occupiers were killed, leaving behind weapons, military equipment, and headquarters documents.

Until March 5, when the town was occupied, Ukrainian defenders steadfastly defended it, inflicting significant losses on the enemy's so-called "elite" units. As a result, during the battles for Hostomel, the Defence Forces of Ukraine managed to gain time to strengthen the capital's defences.

The Russian invaders then tried to build on their success by advancing on Irpin. Our defenders successfully attacked them near the Giraffe shopping centre, destroying 11 enemy BMD-2s. After another attempt to break through the defences, the enemy lost four armoured vehicles and abandoned further assaults on the city from this direction.

However, on March 6, the invaders still managed to break into Irpin from the northwest and took control of almost a third of its territory. The main local thoroughfare, Universytetska Street, became a virtual no-man's land. A fierce four-week battle began for the liberation of Irpin, one of the key suburbs of Kyiv. After capturing the neighbouring towns of Bucha and Hostomel, full control of Irpin would have allowed the invaders not only to get close to the outskirts of Kyiv, but also significantly increased the risk of artillery shelling of the

Destroyed Russian armoured vehicles in Hostomel

Ukrainian defenders of Irpin, who were at the Giraffe position

capital. However, the invaders failed to completely capture Irpin. In particular, after heavy fighting in the area of the Giraffe shopping centre, our forces established control over the central road through Irpin, while the occupiers scattered to the northeastern and southwestern outskirts of the city.

It should be noted that the enemy did not advance a single step closer to our capital in this direction. In fact, the Irpin-Bucha-Hostomel triangle became an impregnable outpost of Kyiv. Fighting continued here for another month. The Irpin River became the main natural barrier on the right bank of Kyiv.

In early March, the enemy's advance was also halted at the line of settlements Kozarovychi – Demydiv – Syniak – Hostomel – Bucha – Berezivka. From the north and west, the capital was surrounded by enemy troops. In addition, the occupiers tried to reach the northern outskirts of Fastiv. It was clear that the enemy intended to create an inner and outer ring of encirclement around the capital. The inner ring was to run along the line of Kozarovychi – Gavrylivka – Hostomel – Bucha – Mykhailivka-Rubezhivka – Stoianka – Horenychi – Yasnohorodka – Lyzhnia – Byshiv – Fastiv, and the outer ring: Ivankiv – Sosnivka – Shybene – Borodchyna – Druzhna – Andriivka – Lynivka – Fasova – Byshiv – Sosnivka – Fastiv. However, due to significant losses in manpower and equipment, the enemy lost the tactical initiative and slowed down its advancc. It failed to carry out its terrible plans to encircle Kyiv.

After a failed attempt at a blitzkrieg in the northeast, the enemy decided to bring all its reserves west of the capital.

Ten of its BTGs, Battalion Tactical Groups, set off along the Borodianka-Makariv-Kalynivka-Vasylkiv-Pidhirtsi route.

The unconquered city of Irpin, March 18, 2022

Destroyed Russian armoured vehicles around Makariv

The occupiers set up checkpoints along the routes to ensure the unhindered passage of their columns and to block supplies to Kyiv. An auxiliary command post, from which Russian troops were directed in the Kyiv direction, was deployed in Chernobyl.

The village of Makariv stood in the way of the enemy's advance, beyond which there was an operational space that allowed them to move along the Zhytomyr highway to Kyiv and begin encircling the capital from the southwest. On February 27, local volunteers engaged in combat on the outskirts of Makariv.

Makariv proved to be a tough nut to crack for the enemy. Unable to capture the village on the move, the occupiers laid siege to it. The forces were unequal: against Russian tanks, Grad multiple rocket launchers, and aircraft, the residents of Makariv had only small arms, a few grenade launchers, and Molotov cocktails.

Vadym Tokar, the head of the Makariv village council, described the situation at the time: "It was especially difficult for the defenders of Makariv because we had no communication with either the district authorities or the capital. We did not know what was happening in the country or where our Armed Forces were."

On March 2, units of the 14th Mechanised Brigade, 95th Airborne Brigade, and Special Forces of the Armed Forces of Ukraine broke through the enemy encirclement and secured their positions in Makariv, where they continued to fight alongside local volunteers against columns of Russian occupiers attempting to break through to the town.

On March 6, Russian troops bypassed Makariv, reached the Zhytomyr highway, and began moving in the direction of Yasynivka-Fastiv. The Russian vanguard advanced to Horenychi. Our command reinforced the defences here with units of the National Guard of Ukraine, anti-tank and rocket artillery. By March 9, the Defence Forces managed to stop the enemy advance on the Yasnohorodka–Horenychi line and successfully hold back the invaders here until almost the end of March. The defenders' artillery prevented the invaders from setting up pontoons and crossing to the right bank of the Irpin River with access to the outskirts of the Sviatoshynskyi district of the capital.

At the same time, the enemy did not abandon its attempts to break through in the Vyshhorod direction. At that time, the line of defence on the right bank of the Dnipro River ran through the settlements of Kozarovychi, Guta-Mezhyhirska, Moshchun, Horenka, Hostomel, Irpin, and Romanivka.

Enemy crossing over the Irpin River destroyed

A natural obstacle stood in their way: the Irpin River.

To cross near Demydiv and Kozarovychi, the enemy brought in up to three BTGs, Battalion Tactical Groups. However, the pontoon bridges they tried to build across the Irpin River were either washed away by the current or destroyed by accurate fire from our artillery. The Russian invaders then focused on breaking through our defences in the area of the village of Moshchun.

This was a promising direction for them, as success would have allowed them to immediately reach the outskirts of the Obolon district of Kyiv.

On March 5, enemy forces in the Vyshhorod direction were reinforced by two marine battalion tactical groups from the Pacific Fleet and special forces units. The invaders decided to use marines and special forces to cross the Irpin River northwest of Moshchun, secure their positions there, and create a bridgehead. They planned to reach the outskirts of Kyiv via Horenka.

To ensure a safe crossing of the Irpin River, Russian invaders launched heavy artillery shelling and air strikes on the village. In total, four of the five enemy pontoon bridges were destroyed by our artillery.

On the night of March 6, Russian marines managed to cross the river and enter the village. The defenders of the village of Moshchun were reinforced by the "Nosorohy" combat group from the Special Operations Forces of the Armed Forces of Ukraine, a unit of the "Azov" Special Forces Brigade of the National Guard of Ukraine, as well as units of the 114th and 112th Territorial Defence Brigades. A fierce battle ensued. Taking advantage of its superior artillery, the enemy fired heavy fire at the village from the area of the villages of Lubianka and

Advance of Russian marines and special forces in the village of Moshchun

Ozer (7–10 km northwest of Moshchun), with unlimited personnel and equipment resources.

Having concentrated up to 200 armoured vehicles and up to 5,000 personnel on the left bank of the Irpin River, the occupiers 6–7 March, they ferried marine and airborne units to the right bank. The defence forces went on the offensive, killing more than 30 Russian marines, but they were unable to completely drive them out of the village. The occupiers occupied the northwestern part of the village. It should be noted that the enemy was well trained and and had combat experience in Syria. On March 7, our artillery fired on Russian troops that had gathered near the crossing in the Moshchun area. Meanwhile, the enemy brought another column of armoured vehicles to the crossing. The column was hit by a powerful artillery strike.

This is how the heavy fighting for control of Moshchun began. The invaders relentlessly pounded Ukrainian positions from the left bank of the Irpin River, while new assault groups in light armoured vehicles entered the village via a pontoon bridge. They tried to break through the defensive lines of our defenders. The enemy captured several bridgeheads on the right bank of the Irpin River and transferred marines and paratroopers there. Enemy reconnaissance UAVs, Unmanned Aerial Vehicle, significantly hampered our artillerymen, who had to protect their few resources. In addition, Moshchun was defended by units equipped with various means of communication, which caused problems with their coordination and even threatened to cut off communication with them. As a result of the enemy's use of electronic warfare, our aerial reconnaissance capabilities using UAVs, Unmanned Aerial Vehicles, were also significantly limited.

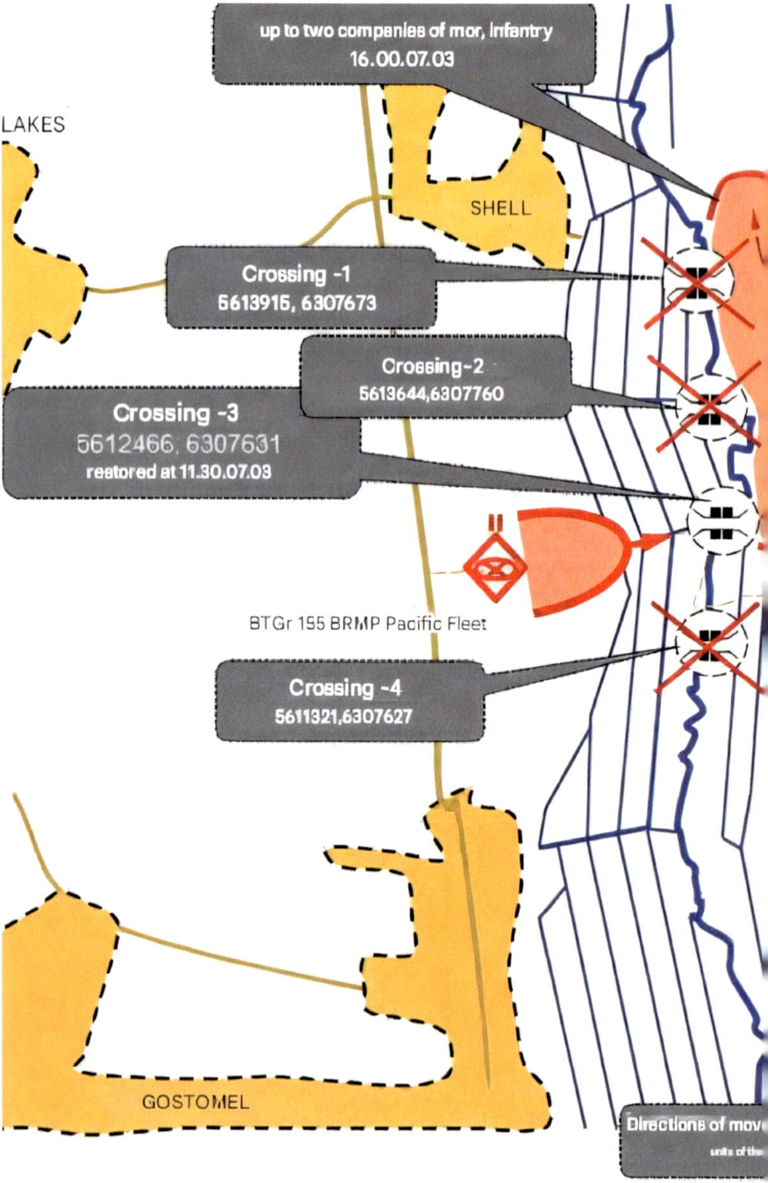

Fig. 4: Defense of the village of Moschunn

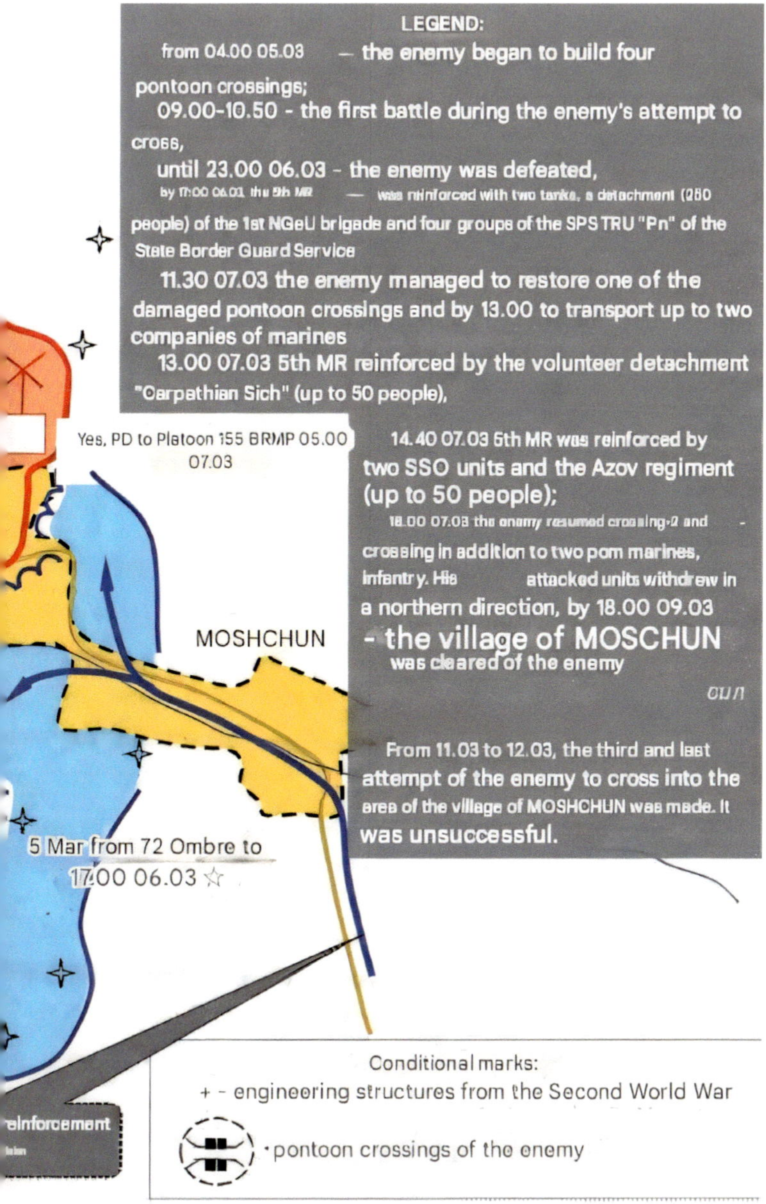
LEGEND:
from 04.00 05.03 – the enemy began to build four pontoon crossings;
09.00-10.50 - the first battle during the enemy's attempt to cross,
until 23.00 06.03 - the enemy was defeated,
by 17:00 06.03 the 5th MR — was reinforced with two tanks, a detachment (250 people) of the 1st NGeU brigade and four groups of the SPS TRU "Pn" of the State Border Guard Service
11.30 07.03 the enemy managed to restore one of the damaged pontoon crossings and by 13.00 to transport up to two companies of marines
13.00 07.03 5th MR reinforced by the volunteer detachment "Carpathian Sich" (up to 50 people),
Yes, PD to Platoon 155 BRMP 05.00 07.03
14.40 07.03 5th MR was reinforced by two SSO units and the Azov regiment (up to 50 people);
18.00 07.03 the enemy resumed crossing-2 and - crossing in addition to two pom marines, infantry. His attacked units withdrew in a northern direction, by 18.00 09.03
- the village of MOSCHUN was cleared of the enemy
MOSHCHUN
From 11.03 to 12.03, the third and last attempt of the enemy to cross into the area of the village of MOSHCHUN was made. It was unsuccessful.
5 Mar from 72 Ombre to 17.00 06.03
einforcement
Conditional marks:
+ - engineering structures from the Second World War
pontoon crossings of the enemy

Realising the complexity of the situation, Colonel General O. Syrskyi personally directed the actions of our units from the command and observation post of the 72nd Mechanised Brigade. Unconventional decisions had to be made.

To make it more difficult for the enemy to cross to the right bank of the Irpin River, the Kyiv Defence Headquarters decided to blow up the dam of the Irpin Water Pumping

Burned Russian armoured vehicles in the village of Moshchun

Schematic layout of the dam on the Irpin River

Station near the village of Kozarovychi. On March 8, our sappers completed this task.

As a result, the water level in Irpin began to rise daily by an average of 0.5–0.7 m, the river spread 2–3 km wide, and the enemy units that had crossed the river found themselves trapped between the river and our defenders and cut off from their main forces.

O. Syrskyi recalled: "A targeted explosion at one of the sluices helped to raise the water level around Moshchun even more. The water rushed in and flooded the Russians, and later we found a place where Russian marines had to throw off all their body armour and swim to stay alive."

On March 11, the invaders launched a massive assault on Moshchun from all sides. Under the influence of the enemy's "fire wall," our defenders were forced to gradually retreat to the outskirts of the village, with their main forces taking up defensive positions in the forest near the village. On March 12, the invaders, supported by artillery, made another unsuccessful attempt to transfer their units from the Chernobyl direction to the Moshchun area. On the same day, near Rakivka, Russian Armed Forces units broke through the defences of the 72nd Mechanised Brigade and crossed the Irpin River, capturing a bridgehead on the left bank of the river. However, Ukrainian artillery destroyed the pontoon bridge, and our special forces isolated and neutralised the occupying forces. Over the next two days, the enemy continued its active offensive under cover of air and artillery strikes from the Moshchun area towards Vyshhorod.

Subsequently, our command brought in additional forces to repel the enemy offensive. After receiving reinforcements, units of the 72nd Mechanised Brigade, together with the National Guard, blocked the village from the

The blown-up dam in the village of Kozarovychi

Remains of Russian marines' equipment

flanks and began shelling the crossing points and concentrations of Russian troops with heavy artillery.

During fierce fighting on March 17, Colonel General O. Syrskyi inspected the defences on the northwestern approaches to the capital in the village of Moshchun and supported our defenders. He noted: "The morale of our defenders is high.

We will destroy the enemy at every opportunity. Russian troops will feel the full fury and strength of Ukrainian defenders."

Such trips were very important for maintaining the morale of the soldiers. Colonel A. Martynov recalls: "At that time, Russian propagandists were flooding our information space with insinuations that the President of Ukraine had fled the country and that we needed to surrender, so the appearance of O. Syrskyi at the front lines had a stabilising psychological effect; the guys understood that their commander was nearby." Two days later, the Defence Forces began pushing the enemy out of the village toward the Irpin River.

On March 21, the village of Moshchun was completely liberated from Russian invaders. This allowed our forces to be redeployed to encircle the enemy group northeast of Irpin.

The defeat of the Russian group in Moshchun was one of the turning points in the battle for the Ukrainian capital. Our soldiers dealt a crushing defeat to the so-called "elite" units of the Russian Armed Forces.

As the President of Volodymyr Zelenskyi emphasised: "By holding Moshchun, we defended the capital. We did not fall. Kyiv stood firm, and with it, all of Ukraine." In the hellish battles for the settlements of Moshchun and Huta-Mezhyhirska, 118 Ukrainian soldiers gave their lives. Glory to the heroes!

Chevrons and uniforms of Russian invaders found after fighting with the occupiers in the village of Moshchun

Colonel General Oleksandr Syrskyi during an inspection of the defence of Moshchun, March 17, 2022

President of Ukraine Volodymyr Zelenskyy presents state awards to participants in the battles for Moshchun

V. Repelling the advance of the ussian federation's armed forces in the Siverskyi operational area

On February 24, the enemy attempted to break through to Kyiv via the Chernihiv and Sumy regions – Siverskyi operational area.

The invaders assigned a special role — that of the "northern gate" — to the Chernihiv region and, in particular, its regional centre. They planned to advance southward along the eastern bank of the Dnipro River near Kyiv in three days. Together with the forces that landed in Hostomel, the enemy intended to completely surround the capital. At the same time, Chernihiv was to become a logistics hub for the enemy, through which the group moving towards the capital would be supplied. The main logistics ar-

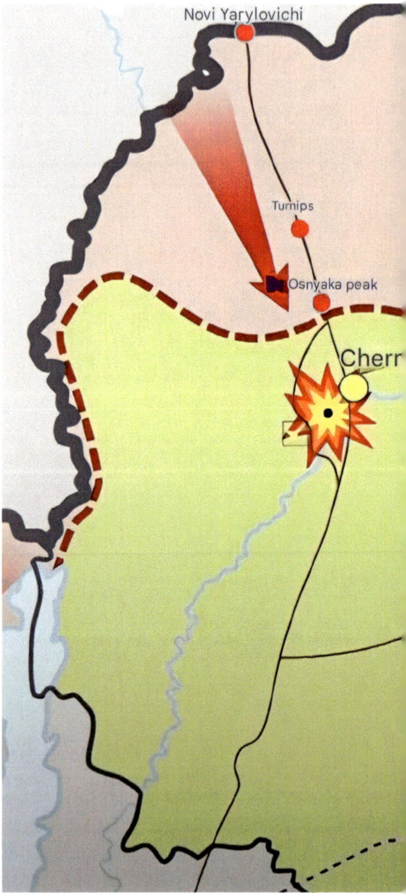

tery was to be the Novi Yarylovychi-Chernihiv-Kyiv highway.

To stop the rapid advance of enemy columns in this direction, at around noon on February 24, our defenders blew up a road bridge across the Dnipro River near the village of

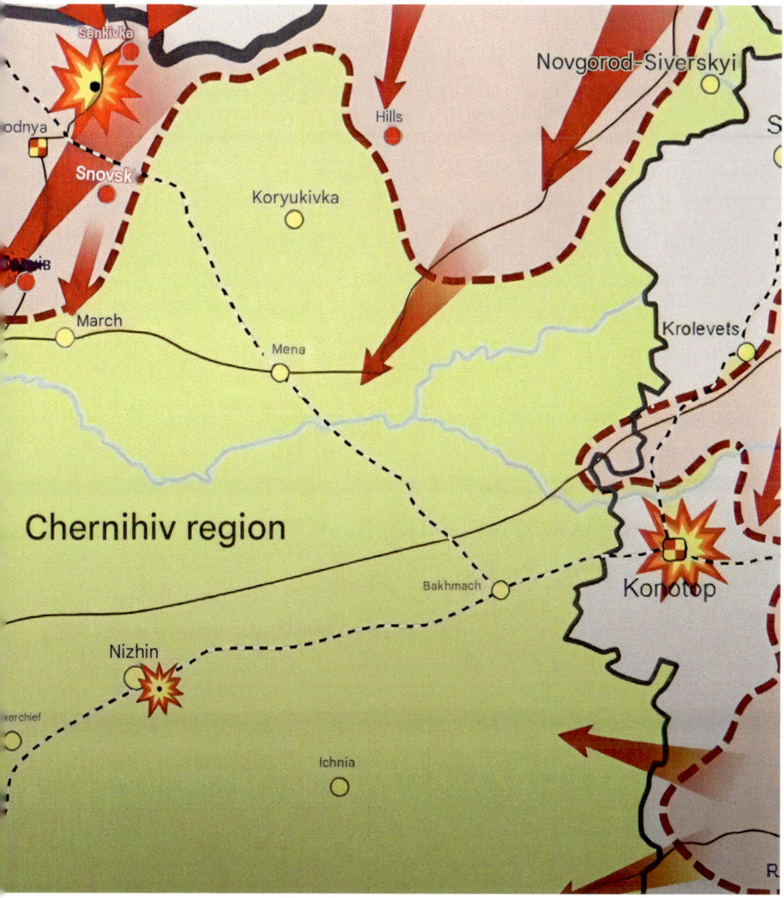

Map of the Russian invasion in the Siverskyi Operational Area

Dniprovske. Since this was the only road between Ukraine and Belarus across the water barrier in the Chernihiv region, our forces managed to stop the movement of enemy convoys here, which gave time to organise the defence on the outskirts of the regional centre. In total, on the first day of the large-scale invasion of the Chernihiv region, about twenty bridges were blown up, anti-tank barriers were set up, and the approaches to the regional centre were mined.

On February 24, the occupiers launched an offensive on the Chernihiv region from several directions simultaneously. From Belarus, they entered through the settlements of Dobrianka and Horodnia in the direction of Ripky, Mykhailo-Kotsiubynske, and Shestovytsia. From the Bryansk region of russia, enemy troops entered Semenivka, Horodnia, Sedniv, and Novhorod-Siverskyi.

A blown-up bridge across the Dnipro River near the village of Dniprovske

According to our military, the largest column of enemy equipment stretched for about 34 km.

On February 24, the occupiers launched an offensive on the Chernihiv region from several directions simultaneously. From Belarus, they entered through the settlements of Dobrianka and Horodnia in the direction of Ripky, Mykhailo-Kotsiubynske, and Shestovytsia. From the Bryansk region of russia, enemy troops entered Semenivka, Horodnia, Sedniv, and Novhorod-Siverskyi.

According to our military, the largest column of enemy equipment stretched for about 34 km.

At that time, the Ukrainian army did not have enough forces to stop the enemy on the border with Belarus, so it was decided to concentrate the available units and firepower to defend the regional centre and switch to mobile defence. As it turned out, the defence of Chernihiv became an important part of the Kyiv defensive operation. Nearly 30,000 Russian troops were opposed by 2,500 Ukrainian defenders.

In preparation to stop the invaders, the Defence Forces of Ukraine regrouped and took up defensive positions to block the main roads used by enemy convoys in the following areas: E95 Chernihiv–Ripky; P12 Chernihiv–Hremiach; P65 Novhorod-Siverskyi–Semenivka. In particular, units of the 1st Separate Brigade advanced to the southwestern outskirts of Chernihiv, with access to combat missions to the north (the planned first line of defence), while units of the 58th Motorised Rifle Brigade from the Sumy direction were concentrated in the southeastern part of the Chernihiv region. Units of the National Guard, Transport Troops, territorial recruitment centers, and the local population set up checkpoints, engineering barriers, and firing positions at the entrances to Chernihiv, Nizhyn, Pryluky, and other settlements. During the defence of Chernihiv Oblast, an interagency headquarters was in operation, which included representatives of all law enforcement agencies responsible for coordination.

The main forces of the 1st OTB were concentrated in the suburbs of Chernihiv. In the first days of the fighting, its units engaged in numerous skirmishes with the enemy, who concentrated his main efforts on the section of the E95 highway between Gomel and Chernihiv. In the Rivnopilia

Units of the 1st OTB on the march

Ukrainian rocket artillery strikes enemy columns in the Rivnopilia area

area, 15 km from Chernihiv, our artillery destroyed two advanced columns of Russian troops. In the Chernihiv direction, units of the 1st OTB managed to stop the enemy in the Baturyn area, as well as on the outskirts of Chernihiv, in Velyki Osniaky and Rivnopilia. On February 25, units of the brigade stopped the superior forces of the occupiers moving from Belarus through Ripky. After receiving a decisive rebuff from our defenders, the enemy was forced to retreat to the northeast of Chernihiv.

In the first days of the large-scale invasion, the enemy lost its tactical advantage, which our defenders took advantage of. Units of the 1st Brigade stopped the enemy's advance vehicles, which were then destroyed by artillery.

At the same time, with accurate strikes on Russian columns, our defenders forced the Russians to turn off the main roads into fields and swamps, where they were de-

Ukrainian artillerymen are hitting the enemy with shells bearing the inscription "For Chernihiv!"

stroyed. "We scattered them and forced them to fight where we wanted them to. We had to lure them away from the border and draw them out. Then we had to inflict damage in small groups, bleeding the main combat units dry," recalled the commander of the 1st Special Forces Brigade, Colonel Leonid Khoda.

The critical moment in the defence of Chernihiv came when enemy tanks broke through to Novoselivka, a strategic hill overlooking the regional centre. At the cost of superhuman efforts, our defenders managed to stop the occupiers and force them to retreat. Another armoured column broke through to Chernihiv from the direction of the Epicenter shopping centre, but was soon destroyed by our tank crews. After that, the occupiers resorted to blockading the city. They took control of all roads leading to Chernihiv, and the fiercest fighting took place northeast of the regional centre near Novoselivka and southeast on the Lukashivka-Kolychevka line. The invaders miscalculated: in the open terrain around Lukashivka, their equipment and supply routes became vulnerable to our artillery. They no longer had sufficient forces to block the regional centre. The courageous resistance of our defenders in this direction halted the enemy's advance and allowed us to gain time to form defences around Chernihiv and the capital.

At the same time, the Russians began a breakthrough in the Sumy direction from the territory of the Bryansk and Kursk regions. During fierce battles, our defenders defended Sumy, Okhtyrka, Lebedyn, Shostka, Konotop, and other settlements. For example, on February 24, the defenders of Okhtyrka: soldiers of the 91st Opos and local volunteers

A damaged Russian tank on the outskirts of Chernihiv

destroyed a military convoy of the so-called "elite" 4th Kantemirovskaya TD, which had entered the city. Subsequently, a unit of the 93rd Mechanised Brigade arrived to assist the defenders of Okhtyrka and successfully attacked another enemy convoy from the 96th Mechanised Brigade. By evening of the same day, our defenders had reached the line of defence on the Sumy-Kharkiv highway, in the direction of Velyka Pysarivka, cutting off the enemy's routes of advance towards Kyiv and Kharkiv.

In Sumy, units of the 81st Airborne Brigade and 117th Brigade of the Troops of the Commander of the 1st Army, together with local residents, twice engaged in combat with enemy columns and forced the occupiers to retreat. Almost 10,000 local residents were armed, which subsequently became a deterrent to Russian intentions to capture this-

Russian equipment burned by defenders of the 93rd Mechanised Brigade

Ukrainian defender of Lebedyn on captured equipment

regional centre. The defenders of Lebedyn also did not surrender to the invaders.

Units of the 81st Airborne Brigade, together with other defenders, bravely held their positions, preventing enemy columns from moving towards Romny and Kyiv.

In Hlukhiv and Konotop, servicemen of the 58th Motorised Brigade. Subsequently, under pressure from superior enemy forces, the brigade's units withdrew southeast of Chernihiv to the Kolychivka-Vertiivka-Bobrovytsia line, where, with small forces on a wide front, they successfully repelled and destroyed enemy columns attempting to break through the regional centre to our capital. Our infantrymen defended Kolychivka in fierce battles and prevented the enemy from breaking through to Chernihiv from the south.

The defenders of Nizhyn, whose core consisted of servicemen of the 219th Engineering Support centre, also distinguished themselves in this direction. With their own forces, they created barricades from trees and mined the enemy's routes of movement. Columns of invaders that stopped in front of such obstacles were successfully destroyed by the city's defenders.

However, the occupiers persistently tried to ensure the maximum advance of their columns along the E95, E391, and H07 highways to the Zalisia-Hoholiv-Boryspil line in order to block Kyiv from the left bank of the Dnipro. To move quickly, the invaders tried to bypass the defensive positions of our troops. As a result, their forces stretched almost 200 km from the border to the outskirts of the capital. In this predominantly wooded area, our units actively attacked and inflicted heavy losses on them.

A logistics convoy was destroyed in the Chernihiv direction

The 72nd Mechanised Brigade destroyed an enemy tank column in the Brovary direction

Under these conditions, the Russian group advancing on Kyiv faced logistical problems, which our defenders took advantage of. Thus, on February 27, thanks to the effective work of the Bayraktar UAV, Unmanned Aerial Vehicle, and our artillery at the Nizkvka station in the Chernihiv region, 56 enemy fuel tanks from the operational reserve of the aggressor's troop group were destroyed. This slowed down their advance and gave our troops time to strengthen their defences, regroup, bring in reserves, and replenish supplies. Subsequent attempts by the enemy to deliver supplies by various means of transport were thwarted by the successful actions of the Defence Forces.

As of March 1, enemy forces advancing from Chernihiv had captured the Kozelets-Bobrovytsia-Makiivka line and later the Svitlynia-Peremoha-Hostroluchia line, reaching a distance of 15-20 km from the city of Brovary. There was a threat of a breakthrough in this direction.

Subsequently, units of the 72nd Mechanised Brigade stopped the enemy's advance on Brovary and Boryspil on the Rusaniv-Hoholiv line. After a failed breakthrough attempt, two enemy BTGs, Battalion Tactical Groups, tried to break out from the northeast towards Rudnia to continue their advance on Brovary.

Under cover of massive artillery fire, the enemy crossed the Trubizh River near the village of Bervytsia with an armoured column of 70 tanks and began moving toward Brovary along the Chernihiv-Kyiv highway. To cover the Brovary direction from the southeast, a mechanised company from the 184th National centre, reinforced by a tank platoon of the 3rd Separate Brigade, was moved to the Yahotyn area.

On March 9, one of the most significant battles in the defence of the capital took place. A column of vehicles from the 6th Tank Brigade of the 90th Tank Division of the invaders moved along the Chernihiv-Kyiv highway with the aim of capturing Brovary and creating a bridgehead for an offensive on Kyiv. In the area of the village of Skibin, the convoy was ambushed by soldiers of the 72nd Mechanised Brigade, the Azov Regiment of the National Guard of Ukraine, and the Territorial Defence Forces. Our defenders were supported by artillery.

The column of enemy vehicles stretched along the highway, with its lead vehicles entering Skibin and the rear still

Destruction of the 6th tank platoon of the 90th tank brigade in the village of Skibin, Brovarskyi district

in the village of Zalissia. The commander of the 3rd battalion of the 72nd Mechanised Brigade, Lieutenant Colonel R. Darmohrai, decided to let the advance guard of 5-6 tanks moving at the head of the convoy pass and strike the main forces.

From a fire ambush set up near the village of Zalissia, our defenders opened fire with Stugna-P anti-tank missile systems and anti-tank grenade launchers on enemy equipment bringing up the rear of the column. Three Russian T-72 tanks were destroyed. The units located on the front line of defence let the column pass as far as possible and began to strike at its flanks. At this time, our artillery began to strike the column. Reconnaissance and fire correction were provided by the skilful use of UAVs, Unmanned Aerial Vehicles.

The enemy had no room to maneuver and was unable to deploy its equipment in battle formation, which was clustered along the road. Armoured vehicles and a TOS-1 flamethrower fired chaotically in all directions, regardless of the civilian population. The crew of one of the damaged Russian tanks managed to launch a smoke screen, making it impossible for our defenders to adjust their artillery fire, and the surviving enemy equipment was able to retreat.

An hour later, the enemy attempted to repeat the attack but suffered heavy losses and retreated. The surviving remnants of the broken column scattered in nearby villages and the Zalissia National Park.

As a result, nearly 30 pieces of enemy equipment were destroyed or damaged, and the tank regiment commander was killed, which led to the loss of the enemy's offensive capabilities.

Military equipment hidden by Russian invaders in the yards of residents of the village of Velyka Dymerka

In the following days, the enemy made several more attempts to resume the offensive on Brovary, but all of them were unsuccessful. It failed to capture the city, but occupied the settlements of Bohdanivka, Zalissia, and Velyka Dymerka.

As of mid-March, Russian invaders had been stopped around Kyiv on both banks of the Dnipro River. Their forces on the right bank of the Dnipro were concentrated in an area that was too narrow for such a large number of units. In addition, the troops were under constant fire from our artillery and suffered heavy losses, which made it impossible to build up forces for a breakthrough. All this created the threat of encirclement of a significant number of enemy troops in the Polissia operational region, and his attempts to launch an offensive from the Siverskyi operational region were unsuccessful. The Defence Forces of Ukraine deployed their reserve units and gradually began to counterattack.

VI. Actions of the air force and air defence during the defence of the Ukrainian capital

The large-scale invasion was carried out by the Russian federation according to a classic scenario and involved an air offensive to destroy all of our air defence systems. The enemy attempted to gain air superiority and ensure the unhindered advance of land forces to encircle Kyiv.

During the first strike, the aggressor fired more than 155 missiles at Ukrainian territory. Our high military command considered various options for striking military targets, but did not expect such a powerful bombardment of civilian infrastructure and the peaceful population. The

Russian missile shot down near Vasylkiv

enemy's psychological pressure on civilians and military personnel to leave their positions and surrender was unsuccessful.

The enemy launched several waves of missile strikes against our radar units, anti-aircraft missile divisions, airfields, and command posts, hoping to gain air superiority and complete control over the situation in the combat zone (blocking the ability to reinforce troops, cutting off logistical supplies, etc.). In the Kyiv direction, such strikes were carried out on the location of the 40th BRTA , OpB – operational brigade, and the positions of the 138th RTBR, (RT Bde, Radio-Technical Brigade) and 96th ZBR, Air Defence Missile Brigade.

The Russian military command focused its efforts on destroying our entire air defence system.

Some foreign experts predicted that our air defence system would survive for between two hours and one day. Despite significant losses in manpower and equipment, the Defence Forces of Ukraine, at the cost of incredible efforts, maintained the combat capability of their units, quickly restored communications and radar stations, and continued to decisively repel the Russian invaders.

To achieve air superiority, the occupiers began literally hunting down our mobile BUK complexes and S-300 installations. However, the anti-aircraft missile forces and aviation of the Ukrainian Air Force carried out constant manoeuvres around Kyiv, thanks to which our air defence system was preserved. Due to the high intensity of the fighting, unit commanders were allowed to make decisions independently depending on the situation.

Kremlin propagandists repeatedly claimed that Ukrainian aviation had been destroyed. However, our pilots were the first to deliver a powerful and unexpected blow to the enemy, taking off from reserve airfields. At that time, Russian planes and helicopters were already in the sky. In groups of 6 to 25 aircraft, the enemy attempted to gain control of the airspace and provide air support to its land forces to quickly capture our territories. The enemy had a 2.5:1 advantage in aircraft. However, the defenders of the Ukrainian sky demonstrated not only extraordinary skill but also exceptional heroism.

The situation in the Kyiv direction was extremely tense. As Lieutenant General A. Kryvonozhko, then Commander of the Air Command "Centre," recalls: "There were 5-6 air

Remains of a downed Russian aircraft

SU-24 of the Ukrainian Air Force during a combat mission

strikes per day, with 2-3 hour breaks between strikes, and attacks intensifying at 3-4 a.m. ... Therefore, our defenders fought around the clock and repelled the enemy with all possible forces. There was no time to rest. Sometimes the personnel didn't even have time to eat, just a quick snack on the go and then back to work. We worked ahead of the enemy, conducting reconnaissance of their further movements and combat operations in order to save as many lives and as much military equipment as possible." Some pilots made three or four sorties a day. They often skipped pre-flight checks and took off from shortened runways that had been bombed, and then repaired at night. The effective work of our Air Force forced the Russian military command to limit the number of sorties of its aircraft and make greater use of its limited supplies of high-precision ammunition.

It was unusual that the main burden of air combat in Ukrainian skies fell on junior officers—military pilots who were mostly senior lieutenants or captains, but demonstrated remarkable courage and a steely spirit. Our fighters and bombers played a key role in stopping the Russian advance on the capital.

To reduce the capabilities of our aviation, the enemy deployed Buk, Tor, Osa, and Tunguska air defence systems around Kyiv. However, they were ineffective in protecting land forces from strikes by our Bayraktar UAVs, Unmanned Aerial Vehicle, and artillery fire, which was coordinated by unmanned aerial vehicles.

Overall, thanks to the timely withdrawal of aviation, anti-aircraft missile and radio-technical forces command posts from enemy strikes, as well as the widespread use of foreign-made portable air defence systems in the Polissia Operational-Strategic Area, we managed to shoot down

Bombing pilots of the Ukrainian Air Force

Russian aircraft shot down near Kyiv by the Air Defence Forces of Ukraine

more than 35% of enemy missiles, prevent the enemy from gaining air superiority, in particular by destroying up to 45% of its combat aircraft and helicopters, and provide air cover for important objects.

In addition to the Ukrainian Air Force, army aviation helicopters delivered powerful strikes against the enemy.

Since the beginning of russia's large-scale aggression, an Army Aviation Control Centre was established at the Command of the Armed Forces of Ukraine for the operational control of army aviation assets.

In the early days of the war, enemy columns moved without air cover, allowing Ukrainian pilots to approach their targets unnoticed, flying at extremely low altitudes. The main targets of their strikes were armoured columns, artillery units, tactical missiles, air defence systems, radar stations, and enemy forward command posts.

Combat sortie of Ukrainian army aviation helicopters

In February and March, our army aviation managed to deliver a number of effective strikes on concentrations of equipment, warehouses of material and technical resources, pontoon bridges, and enemy command posts in the areas of Makariv, Borodianka, Hostomel, and other settlements.

VII. Counteroffensive actions of the Ukrainian Defence Forces. Expulsion of Russian invaders from the occupied territories

By mid-March, through ambushes on enemy advance routes, the Ukrainian Defence Forces managed to disrupt the enemy's logistics system. Convoys of trucks carrying fuel and ammunition were destroyed, and aviation and artillery skilfully struck enemy command posts, warehouses, and other targets.

The invaders' attempts to advance on Kyiv continued until March 19. Since then, Russian troops have exhausted their offensive resources in all directions and have been forced to switch to defence. Our military command managed to stabilise the situation and prevent enemy troops from approaching closer than 25 km (the effective range of field artillery) from the capital. At the same time, the enemy continued rocket attacks and air strikes.

To repel the occupiers from Kyiv and carry out counter-offensive operations, mobile groups were formed from mountain assault, airborne, and mechanised units.

On the left bank of the Dnieper, mountain assault troops advanced to the line of the settlements of Lukianivka, Birky, and Velykyi Krupil, located on the border between the Kyiv and Chernihiv regions. There, they blocked the Kyiv-Sumy highway. Our artillery began striking the outskirts of Ivanivka, southeast of Chernihiv, at the gathering points of Russian military convoys.

At the same time, our paratroopers cut off the supply routes of the 90th Motorised Rifle Division of the Russian Armed Forces and created a so-called operational "pocket." The Russian troops' attempt to break out of the encirclement turned into a panicked retreat and resulted in significant losses for them. As O. Syrskyi recalls: "The landing of our airborne troops was crucial in order to take control of the road junction. This was, I think, in Bobrovytsia, where all the roads supplying the 90th Division converged. Then the command of this group realised that they had fallen into a pocket, almost a cauldron, because they were surrounded by our forces, perhaps and small forces. But it was effectively a ring."

On March 21, during successful operations, the Defence Forces liberated the village of Makariv, drove the enemy out of the Zhytomyr highway, and exposed the rear of Russian troops near Kyiv.

Mountain assault troops of the 109th separate assault battalion of the 10th separate assault brigade in battle near Kyiv

Makariv, liberated from Russian occupiers, March 21, 2022

At the same time, units of the 169th National Guard, advancing in a north-westerly direction, entered enemy-controlled territory and took up positions near the village of Zabuchchia, south-west of the city of Irpin. On March 23, the first reports appeared about the encirclement of Russian forces in Bucha and Irpin, after which our troops pushed the occupiers back to Borodianka and reached the outskirts of the Warsaw highway, which was the main supply line for the enemy. Our defenders' artillery and mobile groups cut off the enemy's supply routes for ammunition, fuel, lubricants, and other supplies. The military operation around Irpin continued for the next few days. The heaviest fighting took place in the area of the Hostomel highway and the military hospital on the northern outskirts of the city. On March 28, Hostomel was liberated.

At the same time, units of the National Guard of Ukraine advanced to the line of Motizhyn–Severinovka–Berezivka–Buzova–Liubymivka and launched a counteroffensive. Over the next three days, they liberated the settlements of Yasnohorodka, Motyzhin, Gorenichi, Kopyliv, Berezivka, and Buzova and pushed the Russian occupiers back beyond the Zhytomyr highway, taking it under their control. Later, on March 30, north of the Zhytomyr highway in the village of Dmytrivka, one of the last large-scale battles in the Kyiv region took place, in which the enemy lost about 18 units of heavy equipment. Two of our tank crews demonstrated their skills and destroyed about 14 units of enemy armoured vehicles.

On the same day, under pressure from our defenders, the occupiers began to retreat from Brovary. Their forces were unable to link up with the group advancing from the Chernihiv direction and were stopped there. The invaders suffered from problems with supplying their group (their logistics were stuck in the Sumy region) and their own mistakes (moving in dense tank columns without infantry and air support). It is important to note the extraordinary support our defenders received from local residents in the Brovary area. Lieutenant Colonel R. Darmohrai, commander of the 3rd battalion of the 72nd Mechanised Brigade, recalled: "As soon as we arrived and began to occupy the defence area, the locals came to our aid. They provided everything from engineering equipment to food. Men came and said, for example, 'I can't fight, I'm not a soldier, but I can dig'. And they dug trenches for several hours. The help from the local population was enormous."

Ukrainian tankers destroyed Russian equipment in the village of Dmytrivka

On the same day, under pressure from our defenders, the occupiers began to retreat from Brovary. Their forces were unable to link up with the group advancing from the Chernihiv direction and were stopped there. The invaders suffered from problems with supplying their group (their logistics were stuck in the Sumy region) and their own mistakes (moving in dense tank columns without infantry and air support). It is important to note the extraordinary support our defenders received from local residents in the Brovary area. Lieutenant Colonel R. Darmohrai, commander of the 3rd battalion of the 72nd Mechanised Brigade, recalled: "As soon as we arrived and began to occupy the defence area, the locals came to our aid. They provided everything from engineering equipment to food. Men came and said, for example, 'I can't fight, I'm not a soldier, but I can dig'. And they dug trenches for several hours. The help from the local population was enormous."

After inflicting serious losses on the occupiers in battles in the Irpin and Brovary directions and cutting off their supply routes, the Ukrainian Defence Forces forced the military and political leadership of the Russian federation to make the shameful decision to retreat their troops back to Belarus and russia. At the same time, having failed to achieve the objectives of the offensive operation, the Kremlin leadership temporarily abandoned the blockade of Kyiv

and ordered the withdrawal of their units from the temporarily occupied northern part of Ukraine. On March 28, the leadership of the Russian Eastern Operational Command instructed all subordinate command posts to provide information cover (legend) for the withdrawal of occupa-

Liberation of Bucha from Russian occupiers, March 31, 2022

tion troops from the captured territories. They were tasked with reporting on the radio about alleged directions of attack and counterattacks, thereby creating the illusion of preparations and the continuation of the offensive.

During the retreat of the occupiers, units of the Ukrainian Defence Forces pursued them (conducting strike and search operations), capturing prisoners and equipment. The enemy underestimated the readiness of our troops to conduct a sustained defence, their early deployment, and the preparation of defensive lines. Most importantly, they did not take into account the massive resistance of the local population.

On March 31, the invaders left Bucha. The next day, they fled from Hostomel, moving through the Chernobyl zone towards Belarus.

On April 2, the Kyiv Regional Military Administration announced the complete liberation of the Kyiv region. By April 5, the Chernihiv region was completely liberated, and by April 11, the Sumy region.

In order to commemorate the feat, mass heroism, and resilience of citizens who defended their cities during the Russian federation's armed aggression against Ukraine, the President of Ukraine issued decrees in March 2022 awarding the cities of Hostomel, Bucha, Irpin, Okhtyrka, and Chernihiv were awarded the honorary title of "Hero City of Ukraine." The successful defence of these cities played a decisive role in the battle for Kyiv.

Conclusions

The main achievement of the Kyiv defensive operation was the foiling of the Kremlin's insidious plans to capture our capital, establish a puppet regime, deprive Ukraine of its independence, and make it a satellite of russia. The victory in this operation allowed our troops to liberate the territories of Zhytomyr, Kyiv, Chernihiv, and Sumy regions.

This operation was carried out in the form of tactical actions by units and military formations. We managed to hold the lines, areas, and positions, as well as objects around Kyiv, thanks to positional defence combined with manoeuvring actions by the troops. In an attempt to reach Kyiv as quickly as possible, the enemy moved in dense armoured columns without infantry or air support, and thus became a target for our mobile groups. The priority task of the Ukrainian Defence Forces, especially at the beginning of the large-scale Russian invasion, was to limit the enemy's mobility by destroying transport infrastructure, in particular bridges and crossings.

It is obvious that the Russian Airborne Forces, which were entrusted with the main tasks during the invasion, were unable to fulfil their direct purpose and were subsequently used as light mechanised units during the hostilities. In addition, the so-called "elite" units of paratroopers and special forces from the Pskov 76th Airborne Division, the Kostroma 98th Airborne Division, the 45th Special Forces Brigade, the 155th Motorised Rifle Brigade, and the

31st Airborne Brigade of the Russian Army ended their campaign ingloriously near Kyiv.

In contrast, the Defence Forces proved themselves quite well in repelling the enemy landing.

The Russians suffered a strategic defeat in the operation, paying dearly for their participation. According to preliminary estimates by military historians, their losses amounted to approximately 10,000 military personnel, approximately 350 tanks, 1,000 armoured combat vehicles, 150 artillery systems, 50 multiple launch rocket systems, nearly 100 aircraft, and 90 combat helicopters.

One of the significant consequences of the defeat of the invaders near Kyiv was a significant psychological effect on the entire Ukrainian society. Since then, our troops have taken the operational initiative and begun the liberation of the occupied territories of Ukraine.

Equally important is that thanks to the successful Kyiv Defence, most world leaders have come to believe in the strength of the Ukrainian people and the power of our army. International support and assistance to our state, including the provision of weapons, ammunition, military equipment, and essential supplies, has become much more active.

List of Abbrivations (NATO-standard English)

Abbreviation	English Designation	NATO-standard Term / Clarification
BpAK	Unmanned Aerial Vehicle	UAV
br Opr	Operational Brigade	Operational Bde
br TA	Tactical Aviation Brigade	Tactical Air Bde
BTGr	Battalion Tactical Group	BTG
BTR	Armoured Personnel Carrier	APC
VIKNU	Taras Shevchenko Military Institute (Kyiv)	Taras Shevchenko Military Inst. (Kyiv)
VITI	Military Institute of Telecommunications & IT (Heroes of Kruty)	Mil. Inst. Telecom & IT (Heroes of Kruty)
GUR	Defence Intelligence Directorate	Main Intelligence Directorate (Defence Intelligence of Ukraine)
DPS	State Border Guard Service	SBGS
DRG	Sabotage and Reconnaissance Group	SRG
DSNS	State Emergency Service	SES
DSV / DShD / PDV	Airborne Forces	Airborne Troops (AF)
ZHVI	Zhytomyr Military Institute (S.P. Koroliov)	Zhytomyr Military Institute (S.P. Koroliov)
ZRB	Air Defence Missile Brigade	Air Defence Missile Bde
ZRK	Air Defence Missile System	ADMS
—	Armed Forces	AFU (Armed Forces of Ukraine)
—	Ministry of Defence	MoD
—	National Guard	NGU
—	National Police	NP
—	Training Centre	TC
—	Separate Airborne Brigade	Sep Airborne Bde
—	Separate Artillery Brigade	Sep Arty Bde
obr SpP	Separate Special-Purpose Brigade	Sep SOF Bde (Special Operations Forces)
obr TrO	Separate Territorial Defence Brigade	Sep TDF Bde
obro GSh	Separate Security Brigade of the General Staff	Sep Security Bde (GS)
obrmp	Separate Marine Brigade	Sep Marine Bde
odshbr	Separate Airborne Brigade	Sep Airborne Bde
ozrp	Separate Air Defence Missile Regiment	Sep AD Regt

ombr	Separate Mechanized Brigade	Sep Mech Bde
ompbr	Separate Motorized Infantry Brigade	Sep Mot Inf Bde
opoz	Separate Regiment for Operational Support	Sep Op Support Regt
oshb	Separate Assault Battalion	Sep Assault Bn
OR	Area of Operations	AO
ORBR	Separate Reconnaissance Brigade	Sep Recce Bde
OTBR	Separate Tank Brigade	Sep Tk Bde
PDD	Airborne Division	Airborne Div
MANPADS	Man-Portable Air Defence System	MANPADS
POPP	Regiment for Operational Purposes	Operational Purpose Regt
PPA	Air Defence	AD
PS	Air Force	AF
rtbr	Radio-Technical Brigade	RT Bde
RT Bde		

List of sources used

1. Koval, M. (ed.). (2023). Year of Indestructibility: The Collapse of Operation Z. Kyiv: NUOU, 320 p.
2. Military-historical description of the Russian-Ukrainian war (February–March 2022). https://milhistory.zsu.gov.ua/voienno-istorychni-opysy
3. Military-historical description of the Russian-Ukrainian war (April 2022). https://milhistory.zsu.gov.ua/voienno-istorychni-opysy
4. A Year of War for Freedom: Military-Historical Sketch of the Russian-Ukrainian War (February 24, 2022–February 24, 2023) in Four Books. (2023). Book I / Office of the Commander-in-Chief of the Armed Forces of Ukraine, General Staff of the Armed Forces of Ukraine, and Centre for Military History Research of the Armed Forces of Ukraine. – Kyiv: Lira-K Publishing House. 270 p.
5. Defence and Liberation of Sumy Region (February–April 2022). https://armyinform.com.ua/2023/03/20/bog-vijny-chernigivshhyna-ta-bilogorivka-try-novi-narysy-vid-czentru-doslidzhen-voyennoyi-istoriyi-zsu/
6. Segeda, S., & Mashtalir, V. (2022). Territorial defence of Ukraine as a phenomenon of national military history. Ukrainian Historical Journal. No. 4. Pp. 148–158. https://doi.org/10.15407/uhj 2022.04.148
7. Kharuk, A. (2022). Defence of the Hostomel and Vasylkiv airfields: an attempt to reconstruct the events. Ukrainian Historical Journal. No. 4. Pp. 139–147. ttps://doi.org/10.15407/uhj2022.04.139
8. Zhirokhov, M. (2022). Northern Outpost. Chernihiv Direction, 2022. Chernihiv: Kniazhyi Val. 69 p.
9. Koval M., Shchypanskyi P., Kidon V., Hrytsiuk V. (2023). The Strategic Nature of the Kyiv Defensive Operation (February 24–April 2, 2022). Ukrainian Historical Journal. No. 3. Pp. 5–29. https://doi.org/10.15407/uhj2023.03.005
10. Piliavets P.I., Sidorov S.V. (2023). The Kyiv defensive operation of 2022: key quantitative and qualitative

indicators. Ukrainian Army: Present and Historical Retrospective: Collection of Materials III International Scientific and Practical Conference. November 23, 2022. Kyiv. Pp. 74–75.

11. Gifts to the Kremlin and scandals in the army: the first major interview with Commander-in-Chief Syrsky/ TSN. tyzhden 19.01.25. https://www. youtube.com/watch?v=WQzUM9-rXF4
12. 24.02: Reconstruction. Oleksandr Syrskyi – Commander of the Land Forces of the Armed Forces of Ukraine (2019-2024), Commander-in-Chief of the Armed Forces of Ukraine (since 2024). https://www.pravda.com.ua/cdn/cd1/reconstruction/a7.html
13. Year of liberation: Kyiv region. https://uinp.gov.ua/informaciyni-materialy/vyzvoleni-regiony-materialy-do-richnyci-deokupaciyi/rik-vyzvolennya-kyyivshchyna
14. The destruction of Wagner, NATO or Sovietism, secrets of the battles for Kyiv and Kursk – how to break military science? https://www. youtube.com/watch?v=VYvM9LxsIIE&t=3503s
15. Tomorrow was war. How Kyiv prepared for defence: new details. https://glavcom.ua/longreads/zavtra-bula-vijna-jak-kijiv-hotuvavsja-do-oboroni-nevidomi-podrobitsi-1046261.html
16. The battle for Kyiv: how it was. The commander of the Land Forces of the Armed Forces of Ukraine, commander of the Kyiv Defence and operational direction, Hero of Ukraine, Colonel General Oleksandr Syrskyi, shared his memories of the details of the Kyiv Defence during the period from February 24 to April 2, 2022. https://armyinform.com.ua/2023/02/16/bytva-za-kyyiv-yak-cze-bulo/
17. Thwarting the Russian offensive on Kyiv: Lieutenant General Anatolii Barylevych recounts the defence of the Hostomel Bridge in 2022 (video). https://pivdenukraine.com.ua/2025/02/25/zirvati-nastup-rosiyan-na-ki%D1%97v-general-lejtenant-anatolij-bargilevich-rozpoviv-pro-oboronu-gostomelskogo-mostu-v-2022-roci-video/
18. Exclusive. Chief of the General Staff Anatolii Barhilevich: "We have only one red line – to preserve Ukraine." https://

glavcom.ua/ longreads/chervona-linija-u-nas-odna-zberehti-ukrajinu-nachalnik-henshtabu-anatolij-barhilevich-eskljuzivne-intervju—1032407.html
19. Thanks to modern aircraft and Western technology, 2023 could be a turning point in Ukraine's war with the aggressor. https://www.facebook.com/GeneralStaff.ua/posts/pfbid0mjJnyBJbvvby6oXGXKUuzpYsvW9pn-VRDk77Rh8QfdMMN7qdKzAuokyaHKqPHJgknl
20. "The Armed Forces of Ukraine destroyed a SOBR convoy": video of the battle has been posted online. https://gazeta.ua/articles/np/_zsu-znischili-kolonu-sobru-u-merezhu-potrapilo-video-boyu/1124401
21. By holding Bakhmut, we are not giving the enemy the opp ortunity to expand the front line, says Syrskyi. https://interfax.com.ua/news/ interview/906054.html
22. "We beat them with experience": how ATO veterans blocked the enemy's path to Irpin. https://armyinform.com.ua/2022/05/20/byly-yih-na-dosvidi-yak-veterany-ato-peretnuly-vorogu-shlyah-do-irpenya/
23. Paul Sonne, Isabelle Khurshudyan, Serhii Morgunov, Kostiantyn Khudov. Battle for Kyiv: Ukrainian valor, Russian blunders combined to save the capital. The Washington Post. 2022. Aug. 24. https://www. washingtonpost.com/national-security/interactive/2022/kyiv-battle-ukraine-survival/?itid=hp-top-table-main-t-2
24. Over 50 occupiers killed in Hostomel in the last two days (18+). https://gur.gov.ua/content/ponad-50-okupantiv-znyshcheno-v-hostomeli-za-ostanni-dvi-doby.html
25. Battle for Kyiv - Part 2 - Animated Analysis. https://www.youtube.com/watch?v=cfX2OLKb_Zw
26. How Irpin was liberated. Chronicle of the Armed Forces of Ukraine counterattack in the northwestern suburbs of Kyiv. https://texty.org.ua/articles/106201/jak-zvilnjaly-irpin-khronika-kontrataky-zsu-u-pivnichno-zakhidnomu-peredmisti/
27. Oleksandr Pavliuk: 70,000 Russians invaded the Kyiv region from Belarus in February 2022. https://www.rbc.ua/rus/news/oleksandr-pavlyuk-70-tisyach-rosiyan-vderlisya-1681132840.html

Image credits

Fig. 1 (page 14f)
Koval M., Schypansky P., Kidon V., Hrytsyuk V. (2023). Strategic nature of the defense operation in Kyiv (February 24 to April 2, 2022). Ukrainian History Journal. No. 3. p. 8.
Fig. 2 (page 18f)
https://armyinform.com.ua/2022/03/21/karta-40-aerodromiv-z-yakyh-rosiya-zdijsnyuye-aviaudary-po-ukrayini/
Fig. 3 (page 21)
https://glavcom.ua/news/komanduvach-oboroni-kijeva-sirskiy-otrimav-geroya-
ukrajini-835821.html#google_vignette
Fig. 4 (page 22)
Kowal M., Schypansky P., Kidon W., Hrytsyuk W. (2023). The strategic nature of Kiev's defense operation (February 24 to April 2, 2022). Ukrainian Historical Journal. No. 3. p. 12., http://resource.history.org.ua/publ/UIJ_2023_3_2
Fig. 5 (page 25), without caption
https://kyiv.comments.ua/ua/news/society/developments/16069-u-kievi-pobilshalo-blokpostiv-nazvana-prichina-foto.html
Fig. 6 (page 27)
https://www.facebook.com/groups/1538271532850784
Fig. 7 (page 28)
https://glavcom.ua/longreads/zavtra-bula-vijna-jak-kijiv-hotuvavsja-do-oboroni-nevidomi-podrobitsi-1046261.html
Fig. 8 (page 30)
https://suspilne.media/275643-osin-bude-virisalnim-periodom-u-vijni-gur/
Fig. 9 (page 31)
https://day.kyiv.ua/photo/terytorialna-oborona-mista-kyyeva-provela-navchannya-svoho-pidrozdilu?page=84&next=1
Fig. 10 (page 32)
https://zn.ua/ukr/UKRAINE/v-ukrajini-planujut-stvoriti-onlajn-muzej-veterana.html
127
Fig. 11 (page 34)
https://www.reuters.com/world/europe/russian-ground-forces-move-closer-kyiv-convoy-stretches-miles-maxar-2022-02-28/

Fig. 12 (page 35)
https://armyinform.com.ua/2023/02/24/hronologiya-rosijsko-ukrayinskoyi-vijny-etapy-vidsichi-vtorgnennya-rf/
Fig. 13 (page 37)
https://rusaggression.gov.ua/ua/rosiiski-okupanty-zaznaiut-nevdachi-u-zakhoplenni-platsdarmu-dlia-nastupu-na-kyiv-a40f719b7821150c8e382b2fee7fcec1.html
Fig. 14 (page 39)
https://www.ukrinform.ua/rubric-regions/3690575-vizvolenna-gostomela-ak-rik-tomu-zsu-znisili-elitnij-rosijskij-desant.html
Fig. 15 (page 41)
https://war.obozrevatel.com/ukr/yakij-viglyad-mae-gostomelskij-aeroport-pislya-boiv-u-genshtabi-pokazali-foto.html
Fig. 16 (page 52)
https://nv.ua/ukr/ukraine/events/bitva-yaka-vryatuvala-kijiv-nv-rekonstruyuvav-istoriyu-zahistu-aeroportu-v-gostomeli-50317852.html
Fig. 17 (page 43)
https://www.5.ua/fotogalereja/shcho-pislia-sebe-lyshaie-putinska-navala-iak-vyhliadaie-vasylkiv-pislia-nichnykh-obstriliv-foto-269461.html
Fig. 18 (page 44)
https://www.facebook.com/permalink.php?story_fbid=707278903935124&id=100039590617894, Andriy Nebitov
Fig. 19 (page 46)
Ukrhydroenergo. https://fakty.com.ua/ua/ukraine/20230608-kyyivska-ges-zahyshhena-vid-udariv-z-povitrya-ta-zseredyny-ukrgidroenergo/
Fig. 20 (page 47)
https://kyiv.comments.ua/ua/news/society/developments/8573-pid-kievom-zbili-sche-odin-boyoviy-vertolit-okupantiv.html
Fig. 21 (page 48)
https://fakty.com.ua/ua/svit/ssha/20220303-ssha-vvazhayut-shho-rosijskyj-vijskovyj-konvoj-pid-kyyevom-vse-shhe-stoyit-na-misczi/
128
Fig. 22 (page 49)
https://www.lsm.lv/raksts/zinas/arzemes/reportaza-cornobilas-atomelektrostacija -sak-apzinat-zaudejumus.a455723/
Fig. 23 (page 50f)

https://www.ukrinform.ua/rubric-ato/3856873-cornobilska-katastrofa-zaporizka-aes-i-okupanti-ak-borotisa-z-adernim-eksgibicionizmom-rosian.html
Fig. 24 (page 52)
https://24tv.ua/kyivnews/zsu-pidirvali-mist-cherez-teteriv-shhob-zatrimati-tehniku-okupantiv_n1878187
Fig. 25 (page 54f)
https://www.bbc.com/ukrainian/features-60747432
Fig. 26 (page 56)
https://war.obozrevatel.com/ukr/gorila-kolona-kemerovskogo-sobru-u-merezhu-potrapilo-video-boyu-na-mostu-cherez-richku-irpin-25-lyutogo.html
Fig. 27 (page 57)
https://war.obozrevatel.com/ukr/gorila-kolona-kemerovskogo-sobru-u-merezhu-potrapilo-video-boyu-na-mostu-cherez-richku-irpin-25-lyutogo.html
Fig. 28 (page 59)
https://www.youtube.com/watch?v=sdDD-s0Dacg, video screenshot
Fig. 29 (page 60)
https://novynarnia.com/2022/02/26/shhob-vorog-ne-prorvavsya-do-kyyeva-z-boku-zhytomyrshhyny-pidryvayut-mosty-ye-zhertvy/
Fig. 30 (page 61)
https://www.radiosvoboda.org/a/news-kyiv-viiskova-komendatura/31779641.html
Fig. 31 (page 62)
https://www.radiosvoboda.org/a/news-kyiv-viiskova-komendatura/31779641.html
Fig. 32 (page 63)
https://day.kyiv.ua/photo/terytorialna-oborona-mista-kyyeva-provela-navchannya-svoho-pidrozdilu?page=84&next=1
Fig. 33 (page 64f)
Kowal M., Schypansky P., Kidon W., Hrytsyuk W. (2023). The strategic
nature of Kiev's defense operation (February 24 to April 2, 129
2022) . Ukrainian Historical Journal. No. 3. p. 12. , http://resource.history.org.ua/publ/UIJ_2023_3_2
Fig. 34 (page 66)
https://armyinform.com.ua/2022/03/14/blokpost-pid-komanduvannyam-desanta/

Fig. 35 (page 67)
https://armyinform.com.ua/2022/05/20/byly-yih-na-dosvidi-yak-veterany-ato-peretnuly-vorogu-shlyah-do-irpenya/
Fig. 36 (page 69)
https://mig.com.ua/henshtab-zsu-pro-oriientovni-vtraty-voroha-na-21-veresnia-640920-1440-osib-1193-4-rszv-18270-58-artsystem/
Fig. 37 (page 70)
https://texty.org.ua/articles/106201/jak-zvilnjaly-irpin-khronika-kontrataky-zsu-u-pivnichno-zakhidnomu-peredmisti/
Fig. 38 (page 71)
https://glavred.info/ukraine/bitva-pod-kievom-voydet-v-uchebniki-po-voennoy-istorii-veteran-ssha-10374384.html
Fig. 39 (page 72)
https://mig.com.ua/henshtab-zsu-pro-oriientovni-vtraty-voroha-na-21-veresnia-640920-1440-osib-1193-4-rszv-18270-58-artsystem/
Fig. 40 (page 73)
https://glavred.info/ukraine/bitva-pod-kievom-voydet-v-uchebniki-po-voennoy-istorii-veteran-ssha-10374384.html
Fig. 41 (page 74)
https://glavred.info/ukraine/bitva-pod-kievom-voydet-v-uchebniki-po-voennoy-istorii-veteran-ssha-10374384.html
Fig. 42 (page 75)
https://www.facebook.com/story.php?story_fbid=263905492587545&id=1000
69042885845&__mmr=1&_rdr
Fig. 43 (page 77)
https://cripo.com.ua/main/yak-selishhe-makariv-malimi-silami-vistoyalo-proti-rosijskoyi-navali/
Fig. 44 (page 77)
https://edition.cnn.com/europe/live-news/ukraine-russia-putin-news-
03-13-22/index.html
130
Fig. 45 (page 78)
https://www.youtube.com/watch?v=PVeQFh-wDMU
Fig. 46 (page 80f)
https://detector.media/kritika/article/209074/2023-03-18-zhyty-v-kostromi-pomerty-v-moshchuni/

Fig. 47 (page 82)
https://ua.korrespondent.net/ukraine/4465911-moschun-ruiny-i-trupy-rosiian-fotoreportazh-18
Fig. 48 (page 83)
https://detector.media/kritika/article/209074/2023-03-18-zhyty-v-kostromi-pomerty-v-moshchuni/
Fig. 49 (page 84)
https://uk.wikipedia.org/wiki/%D0%9F%D1%96%D0%B4%D1%80%D0%B8%D0%B2_%D0%9A%D0%BE%D0%B7%D0%B0%D1%80%D0%BE%D0%B2%
Fig. 50 (page 85)
https://argumentua.com/stati/yak-zsu-rozbili-el-tu-put-nsko-arm-u-moshchun-ta-zupinila-nastup-na-ki-v-rozsl-duvannya
Fig. 51 (page 86)
https://ru.krymr.com/a/v-rossiyskoy-armii-zastavlyayut-voyevat-ranennykh-i-kalek/33459004.html
Fig. 52 (page 87o)
https://www.ukrinform.ua/rubric-kyiv/3432350-komanduvac-suhoputnih-vijsk-pereviriv-oboronu-najgaracisogo-napramku-kieva.html
Fig. 53 (page 87u)
https://www.president.gov.ua/news/zvilnennya-moshuna-stalo-odnim-iz-povorotnih-momentiv-nashoy-81705
Fig. 54 (page 88 f)
Chernihiv Region Prosecutor's Office, https://www.facebook.com/100067065800771/posts/5020472224742229/
Fig. 55 (page 90)
https://suspilne.media/chernihiv/246330-persi-prijnali-udar-rosian-ak-zgaduut-podii-24-lutogo-prikordonniki-z-dniprovskogo/
Fig. 56 (page 92)
https://defence-ua.com/photo/1_a_tankova_brigada_zsu_z_chernigivschini_vidpratsjuvala_vidbittja_ataki_ta_blokuvannja_protivnika-123.html
131
Fig. 57 (page 93)
https://odessa.online/u-genshtabi-zsu-oprilyudnili-operativnu-informatsiyu-z-frontu-150/
Fig. 58 (page 94)

https://suspilne.media/chernihiv/398846-but-voroga-snaradami-za-cernigiv-reportaz-z-pozicij-artileristiv-1-tankovoi-brigadi/
Fig. 59 (page 95)
https://www.radiosvoboda.org/a/zhyteli-chernihova-pro-pershi-dni-povnomasshtabnoho-vtorhnennya/32827834.html
Fig. 60 (page 96)
https://novynarnia.com/2022/03/02/93-tya-brygada-2/
Fig. 61 (page 97)
https://armyinform.com.ua/2023/06/24/oborona-sumshhyny-abo-yak-lebedyn-stav-kladovyshhem-dlya-rosiyan/
Fig. 62 (page 98)
https://t.me/uniannet/36074
Fig. 63 (page 99)
https://militarnyi.com/uk/news/chorni-zaporozhtsi-pid-brovaramy-rozbyly-bronetehniku-rosiyan/
Fig. 64 (page 101)
https:// t.me/Pravda_Gerashchenko/3110
Fig. 65 (page 102)
https://nv.ua/ukr/ukraine/politics/ yak-perezhila-rosiysku-okupaciyu-velika-dimerka-u-brovarskomu-rayoni-viyna-rosiji-proti-ukrajini-50233028.html#goog_rewarded
Fig. 66 (page 104)
https://suspilne.media/543559-rosia-obstrilue-ukrainu-raketami-aki-23-roki-tomu-kiiv-viddav-moskvi/
Fig. 67 (page 106)
ZSU. https://www.unian.ua/war/ekspert-poyasniv-chomu-aviaciya-rf-ne-z-yavlyayetsya-v-nebi-ukrajini-novini-vtorgnennya-rosiji-v-ukrajinu-11934333.html
Fig. 68 (page 107)
https://shotam.info/z-iavylysia-unikalni-kadry-boyovoi-roboty-ukrainskoho-bombarduvalnyka-su-24m-video/ Dmytro Muravsky
Fig. 69 (page 108)
https://armyinform.com.ua/2023/11/21/lotchyk-bombarduvalnyk-pro-znyshheni-kolony-okupantiv-vorozhi-raketni-udary-po-aerodromah-ta-poloty-na-granychno-malyh-vysotah/
Fig. 70 (page 109)
https://kyiv.ukrainianwall.com/uk/87349-navit-ne-vstig-vidstrilyatisya-nashi-suhoputni-viyska-nagnuli-do-zemli-lastivku-okupantiv-video-raduye-ukrajinciv

Fig. 71 (page 110)
https://armyinform.com.ua/2023/04/10/derzhava-terorystne-zdolaye-yednosti-vsih-hto-czinuye-svobodu-volodymyr-zelenskyj/
Fig. 72 (page 112)
https://zahid.espreso.tv/ vijskovi-lviv-vid-oboroni-kiivshchini-do-boiv-za-bakhmut-ta-limanskiy-napryamok-boyoviy-shlyakh-109-batalyonu-10-ogbshr-edelveys
Fig. 73 (page 113)
https://shepetivka.com.ua/novyny/podii/10231-viina-rosii-proty-ukrainy-sytuatsiia-stanom-na-ranok-22-bereznia-2022-roku.html
Fig. 74 (page 115)
https://www.village.com.ua/village/city/picture-story/325193-reportazh-iz-dmitrivki
Fig. 75 (page 116)
https://hmarochos.kiev.ua/2022/04/01/mer-buchi-zayavyv-pro-zvilnennya-mista-vid-rosijskyh-okupantiv/

BERLIN STORY VERLAG Schöneberger Straße 23 A | 10963 Berlin

Enno Lenze

INTO THE FIRE

Reports from crisis areas
372 pages, 112 illustrations, 12.5 x 19 cm, paperback, €20
Order at: berlinstory-buch.de/p/into-the-fire-english

Enno Lenze, Lenze, head of the Berlin Story Bunker, was on his way to Bucha when this place was not yet synonymous with Russian war crimes. He reports from the front lines in Ukraine, from the fight against ISIS in the Autonomous Region of Kurdistan, from the Taliban in Afghanistan, and from tear gas attacks on students in Hong Kong. He covers arms fairs in Paris and Dubai as well as the attempted storming of the Bundestag by Reich citizens.

Paul Ronzheimer, war reporter, Journalist of the Year 2022, deputy editor-in-chief of BILD, got to know Enno Lenze through Kurdistan. They met in Ukraine and missed each other in Afghanistan.Paul Ronzheimer reports daily on Twitter (like Enno Lenze) and in the RONZHEIMER podcast.

The Cover

The cover photo shows Enno Lenze on the highway to Bucha on April 2, 2022, the day the Russians lost the battle for Kyiv and withdrew. „We pass destroyed bridges and see riddled civilian cars. Some are perforated like a colander. Behind the cars are the first corpses. Then an ambulance, riddled with ammunition and shrapnel. In the cars are the bodies of men, women, and children. A Lada is facing the wrong way on the road, with a body behind it. A person who had sought shelter behind the car, shot and then run over. I see a hundred kilometers of Russian war crimes.“

About the author

Enno Lenze is socially engaged in a variety of ways in the areas of refugee aid, education, and teaching German history. He regularly travels to war and crisis zones himself to report from there, but also to carry out his own aid projects.

WWW.BERLINSTORY.DE